Calling All Angels

*An Advent Study
of Fearlessness and Strength*

Erin Wathen

*Life begins at the end of your
comfort zone*

WJK WESTMINSTER
JOHN KNOX PRESS
LOUISVILLE • KENTUCKY

First edition
Published by Westminster John Knox Press
Louisville, Kentucky

24 25 26 27 28 29 30 31 32 33—10 9 8 7 6 5 4 3 2 1

Book design by Drew Stevens
Cover design by Mary Ann Smith
Cover art by Daniel Bonnell. Used by permission.

Library of Congress Cataloging-in-Publication Data

Names: Wathen, Erin, author.
Title: Calling all angels : an Advent study of fearlessness and strength / Erin Wathen.
Description: 1st edition. | Louisville, Kentucky : Westminster John Knox Press, [2024] | Summary: "Diving into the stories of the Gospels' angelic appearances as well as other Scriptures calling us to live courageously, Erin Wathen offers weekly and daily readings that call us to overcome our fears in order to live more fully as followers of Christ"-- Provided by publisher.
Identifiers: LCCN 2024024187 (print) | LCCN 2024024188 (ebook) | ISBN 9780664268978 (paperback) | ISBN 9781646984015 (ebook)
Subjects: LCSH: Angels. | Advent--Prayers and devotions. | Christmas--Prayers and devotions.
Classification: LCC BL477 .W354 2024 (print) | LCC BL477 (ebook) | DDC 242/.33--dc23/eng/20240627
LC record available at https://lccn.loc.gov/2024024187
LC ebook record available at https://lccn.loc.gov/2024024188

Most Westminster John Knox Press books are available at special quantity discounts when purchased in bulk by corporations, organizations, and special-interest groups. For more information, please e-mail SpecialSales@wjkbooks.com.

For Grace Immanuel,

the most fearless church I know

Calling All Angels provides a wealth of resources for group study and worship for the Advent season. To enhance your use of this book, digital resources, including images for displaying during worship services or group sessions, a Spotify playlist, and chapter introductions from the author are available at **www.wjkbooks.com/CallingAllAngels**.

CONTENTS

INTRODUCTION

"Do not be afraid."
     It's the most frequently repeated message in Scripture.

Some say it appears 365 times, to be exact. That sounds a bit too much like a marketing team decided they'd found a great idea for a Christian daily devotional . . . one text a day for a calendar year, what are the odds!?

But even if the actual math is not quite that convenient, some variation of "fear not" really does come up more than three hundred times in the Bible. From Genesis to Revelation; from the prophets to the psalms; from Jesus to the faithful ones who followed, the words have become a mantra across time and space. Clearly faith cannot thrive when fear is in charge. Maybe that's why some of the most awe-inspiring expressions of this message appear in the Gospel stories leading up to Jesus' birth. Angelic beings appear several times preceding the nativity story to those who are awaiting this blessed event—whether they know it or not yet—and each time, the angels bear the same memo: do not be afraid. The primary origin story of our faith insists and relies on this compelling refrain: let go of your fear, and amazing things will follow.

Years ago, I attended a leadership event where the facilitator started out with a simple question for the participants to discuss in small groups: What would you do if you weren't afraid?

The exploration of that question turned out to be a game changer in my life—for the space of that event and ever since. In the years since that gathering, I have held up that same question, for myself and for others, in various contexts. In a moment when the path forward doesn't seem clear, when there seems to be no right answer, or when my own wisdom is obviously insufficient, to begin from a place of fearlessness almost always provides a turning point, even if that courage is hypothetical at first! Whether in a professional, personal, communal, or spiritual setting, asking ourselves what we'd do if we were truly unafraid provides a filter that can distill even the most difficult moment of stuckness to a moment of truth.

The trick is that you can't begin to answer that question until you first start naming what you are afraid *of*. It's amazing how much power fear can hold over a person or institution if that fear has never been acknowledged or articulated. But once you start to get to the root of what fears have been calling the shots, you can decommission them. And then the whole sky opens up.

Considering the number of biblical reminders on the topic, perhaps people of faith should adopt this as our leading question for all of life: What would we do if we weren't afraid? What would change in our relationships, in our vocations, in our congregations—maybe even in our communities and in our world—if God's people led with a courage and vision that was always, first and foremost, unafraid? If we could not be bullied by bigots or confined by the bounds of capitalism? If we were undeterred by threat of violence or rumors of war? If the suffering of the world never sent us into petrified despair, but only ever inspired us to courageous action?

With some intention on our part, the Advent season can be a time of manifesting that kind of transformational courage. Where better to find the strength, hope, and fearlessness than in the lives of those who first witnessed the coming of Christ?

In these iconic episodes leading up to Jesus' birth, angels visit trembling mortals (who, to be fair, are having a totally normal human reaction to an encounter with otherworldly beings). The angels offer those mortals a glimpse of the new, world-changing thing that God is about to do, and then they invite said mortals to participate in this story in some way.

Who is on the receiving end of these Advent tidings?

— An aged priest who—impossibly—is about to become a father for the first time.
— A young woman who is about to become a mother, without the safety and protection of marriage.

— A simple carpenter who is asked to do the unconventional, the unthinkable, the impossible — setting aside everything he knows about family, values, and life.
— A group of ordinary shepherds who are just out minding their ordinary sheep — and about to get the extraordinary fright of their lives!

Into each of these human stories comes an in-breaking of some fearful reality. But over each of them, the same call is spoken or sung: *do not be afraid.*

In theory, that is wonderfully comforting and empowering. In practice, of course, we know from our own experience that it is easier said than done. Some quick doomscrolling in the morning with our coffee reminds us just how much there is to fear: how much uncertainty, how many enemies, how little truth, and how deep the mistrust of our neighbors.

The imminent dangers of climate change are real. The escalating gun violence and the duplicitous politicians are real too. So are the global conflicts, the refugee crisis, the growing gap between rich and poor, and the increased frequency and severity of natural disasters. Pile these onto our own addictions, struggling relationships, difficult jobs, and health challenges and we may find ourselves wondering: *Where are our angels?*

The angels of the biblical Christmas story too often become relics of a romanticized past and a nostalgia-heavy holiday culture. They are the things of Hallmark cards, TV musicals, church Christmas pageants, and your country mamaw's wall decor. No offense intended—I love a country mamaw and everything about her—but somewhere along the way, we've diminished the power of that angelic voice with our seasonal renderings. We cherish angels among the cast of nativity characters, but do we perhaps fail to hear their call—*do not be afraid!*—as the declaration of resistance that it is? Their ancient chorus is not just a gentle reminder but a firm command, one that is not to be ignored but most definitely needs to be reckoned with.

The world needs that timeless message of courage more than ever, rearranged for a new season, turned up and tuned in to the needs of this moment. Surely the pervasive call of "fear not" that rings throughout the whole arc of Scripture still echoes today.

Historically, fear has often been wielded as a weapon by insecure faith leaders. The language of sin and judgment, alongside images of a vengeful God, can serve as both a recruiting tool and a manipulative means of control. As people leave organized religion in droves, we are seeing the tragic fallout of this "brand" of faith. People are reckoning with the trauma wrought by toxic theology and realizing that they would rather live unafraid than bound by the ancient tropes of church. The irony is that the Christian faith actually contains within its narrative the power to dismantle and dispel all fear! Fearless faith can transform lives, and the world. This is the true spirit of the gospel of Jesus Christ: healer, liberator, and miracle worker.

In anticipation of Christ's birth, we gather around the stories that have empowered generations of faithful witnesses to that liberating love.

In the face of the fearful uncertainty of the modern world, we will rally with the courage and strength that the gospel has always contained. In the hopeful spirit of Advent, we will hear and repeat the angels' invitation for our time. The sacred call and response appears in Scripture often enough that we should understand the assignment by now. "Do not fear" is not just a comforting phrase; it is an invitation and a commissioning.

Once we begin the work of Advent, we become Advent *people*: people of good faith who acknowledge the deep anxiety of the world, and of our time in particular. People aware of the source of deep human fear but never bound by it, present to the suffering and need of the world but not crippled by its enormity. Advent people are rooted in reality but live as those who've been fearlessly empowered by the Spirit to be justice-seeking, peace-loving witnesses to the new thing God is doing in creation.

How will we spend these days of waiting for Christ to be born among us? If we answer the angels' call, we will spend this time acting on our hope and not our fear. We will proclaim peace when the world shouts its collective anxiety. We will live joyfully undeterred by the powers of evil and always, always embody love instead of letting that four-letter f-word lead the way.

You know the one: fear.

I pray that these Advent reflections will serve as a resource for your courageous living. Each chapter features a thematic introduction for the week based on the story of an angelic encounter surrounding the birth of Jesus, followed by questions for personal reflection or group discussion, an activity suggestion, and five daily reflections. There is also a Christmas chapter with questions for your personal reflection or journaling, but there are no daily reflections for that week. At the end, you'll find liturgy content, including original readings for Advent candle lighting and Christmas Eve. And because this season calls for music, there is a suggested playlist—which I suggest you check out sooner than later—to provide a soundtrack for the journey. See page 139 and visit https://spoti.fi/3K230It.

May this journey toward fearlessness help you find hope, peace, joy, and love along the way, and may you share it with a neighbor or a stranger. May the skies open up as you wait for God to do a new thing, in your life and in the world.

But first, take just a moment and ask yourself: What would you do if you weren't afraid?

FIRST WEEK OF ADVENT

Let All Mortal Flesh Keep Silent

We are socially programmed to fear silence. Awkward silence in a conversation? Fill it with an even more awkward joke or inappropriate comment! What about the silence of an empty house: Can we be still and enjoy it, or do we suddenly remember the hundred things we have to do or, maybe, go and buy? A quick scroll of the newsfeed (which, if we're being honest, is rarely a quick scroll at all) is filled with sound-bite boobytraps just waiting to interject a loud and jarring interruption into our meeting or worship service, revealing that we've been on our phone when perhaps we shouldn't be. Endless reels intrude with the sudden noise of advertising, social commentary, cooking, or funny animal videos unless we remember to hit the mute button in time.

In the same vein, it seems we've effectively filled the silences of nature with the sounds of construction and traffic. In fact, in certain seasons, the most beautiful natural spaces imaginable are the ones most full of people and cars! Yosemite, the Grand Canyon, the beach, any local or state wonder designated as an area of refuge . . . you can enjoy the views, but prepare to enjoy them with a few thousand of your closest friends and their vehicles.

My home state of Kentucky boasts the natural wonder that is Mammoth Cave National Park. On a guided walk through the caves, there is a point at which the guide will invite you to stop. The guide will then turn off the light. You have reached a point so deep in the heart of the earth that it is truly and completely devoid of light or sound. The guide will invite everyone to stand still for just a moment and experience the true sensory deprivation of this natural wonder. It is wicked weird. It is also a blessed relief from the chaos of the aboveground world. By the time the guide turns the light back on, you've gotten over the weirdness and might find yourself wishing that you could stay awhile, the ancient limestone walls providing sanctuary from all the noise of your life.

In fact, legend has it that there was a time when local congregations would gather in those rocky depths for their summer worship services. The cave was a great place to keep cool in the days before churches had such a thing as air conditioning. That's how the story goes, anyway: the dark, cool space was inviting enough to entice folks from their labors in the sun and into a place of (blessedly cool) worship. And while I'm sure respite from the heat was a blessing in itself, I'd venture that the sacredness of the space can be attributed most to its silence: a true sanctuary in every sense of the word.

The pervasiveness of sound in the modern age has made us averse to anything resembling true silence. Even when we do seek out a silent sanctuary, we may find that our inner dialogue remains on at HIGH VOLUME, so long has it been since we experienced external quiet. Without any hard data to footnote here, I'm going to venture a hunch that this is largely an adverse effect of late-stage capitalism. The noisier our surroundings, the more likely we are to lose touch with the inner life of the spirit and the more vulnerable we become to engaging in gross consumption. And what's good for commerce is usually terrible for the human spirit.

Enter the prophets of our ancient story, and the prophets of today. Prophets speak truth to power, challenge us to act for justice, and rail against broken systems that harm the vulnerable. They can be loud. But prophets also sometimes invite us to a quieter way. They call us to lean into silence—not just to stop speaking, but to find and embody an inner quiet of the spirit that makes space for transformation.

Some prophets model silence as a spiritual practice. From the desert mothers to more contemporary figures like Thomas Merton, prophetic voices remind us that spiritual practices of prayer and contemplation are essential for the work of justice, calling us back to our humanity when the world has fractured it.

Silence can be an intentional discipline in the life of faith; silence can also be an enforced reality by some circumstance beyond our control. And at times when the spirit is most in need of it, silence might even come by way of divine intervention.

Zechariah's Angel

In the days of King Herod of Judea, there was a priest named Zechariah, who belonged to the priestly order of Abijah. His wife was descended from the daughters of Aaron, and her name was Elizabeth. Both of them were righteous before God, living blamelessly according to all the commandments and regulations of the Lord. But they had no children because Elizabeth was barren, and both were getting on in years.

Once when he was serving as priest before God during his section's turn of duty, he was chosen by lot, according to the custom of the priesthood, to enter the sanctuary of the Lord to offer incense. Now at the time of the incense offering, the whole assembly of the people was praying outside. Then there appeared to him an angel of the Lord, standing at the right side of the altar of incense. When Zechariah saw him, he was terrified, and fear overwhelmed him. But the angel said to him, "*Do not be afraid*, Zechariah, for your prayer has been heard. Your wife Elizabeth will bear you a son, and you will name him John. You will have joy and gladness, and many will rejoice at his birth, for he will be great in the sight of the Lord. He must never drink wine or strong drink; even before his birth he will be filled with the Holy Spirit. He will turn many of the people of Israel to the Lord their God. With the spirit and power of Elijah he will go before him, to turn the hearts of parents to their children and the disobedient to the wisdom of the righteous, to make ready a people prepared for the Lord." Zechariah said to the angel, "How can I know that this will happen? For I am an old man, and my wife is getting on in years." The angel replied, "I am Gabriel. I stand in the presence of God, and I have been sent to speak to you and to bring you this good news. But now, because you did not believe my words, which will be fulfilled in their time, you will become mute, unable to speak, until the day these things occur."

Meanwhile, the people were waiting for Zechariah and wondering at his delay in the sanctuary. When he did come out, he was unable to speak to them, and they realized that he had seen a vision in the sanctuary. He kept motioning to them and remained unable to speak. When his time of service was ended, he returned to his home.

After those days his wife Elizabeth conceived, and for five months she remained in seclusion. She said, 'This is what the Lord has done for me in this time, when he looked favorably on me and took away the disgrace I have endured among my people."

—Luke 1:5–25; emphasis added

Zechariah is alone in a holy place when Gabriel—the archangel dispatched as messenger of God—appears to him. That backdrop alone is significant. The priest has been sent to perform the ritual burning of incense while the whole assembly prays outside the sanctuary. You can almost hear the stark contrast between the outer world—the buzz and chatter of a congregation awaiting worship—and the relative dark and stillness of the empty sanctuary just inside the doors.

Having been removed from the crowd, in the silence of that sanctuary, a space has been carved out of ordinary life for Zechariah to have an extraordinary encounter. An angel appears with a life-changing message. This is a recurring theme throughout the Gospel of Luke, as angels appear frequently to announce, instruct, guide, and protect. Though rare in early Judaism, angels became more common in later eras as mediators between God and humans.[1]

It seems that in this case, silence and solitude are almost prerequisites for a significant act of the Holy. Perhaps we can take a hint for today as well: removing oneself from noise and distraction often clears the way for divine encounter.

In the space of that silence, the angel speaks a word of life-changing, unbelievable good news. Zechariah's wife, Elizabeth, will give birth to a child. That's the life-changing part. The unbelievable part is that Elizabeth has long passed what even modern medicine would consider child-bearing age. What the angel proposes is preposterous! Zechariah has some questions, as would anyone.

The news that the angel has just delivered is certainly significant, not just for the lives of Elizabeth and Zechariah, but in the whole arc of the biblical story. Like Sarah and Abraham before them, the couple has waited for many years for God to give them a child. It was a dream long deferred and then abandoned entirely—they had now reached an age at which it would be impossible for them to have a baby—literally, physically, biologically impossible.

And yet.

This pair is about to enter a season in which God does new and surprising things, when the impossible becomes possible. Again Zechariah has big questions! But it turns out those questions are not the right ones. Because following the initial conversation with God's celestial agent, the prophet is stricken silent.

It seems that the correct response to news so wonderful, impossible, mysterious, and truly awesome is to simply shut up. And thus the priest/prophet/father-to-be is essentially sentenced to a nine-month time out. (Note to self: if a messenger of God comes bearing gifts, you say thank you and then hush!)

It's probably for the best that Zechariah came down with long-term laryngitis. Otherwise, he might have run right home to blurt out the same sort of things to his *wife* that he just said to the angel! Can you imagine? Just picture Zechariah going home and saying to Elizabeth: *Come on now, I believe in the Lord's mighty powers and all, but you are no spring chicken!* Certainly the angel took the priest's voice away to teach him a lesson about his unbelief; but it may have also kept the priest out of trouble with his spouse in a more immediate and practical sense!

Talking too much, as most of us well know, can lead to all sorts of trouble. It can also distract us from the significance of the moment at hand.

As is often the case, it is important to take a step back from the text and acknowledge some problematic themes. Particularly the belief of the ancients (and not-so-ancients) that fertility was closely tied to God's favor. Much like the prosperity gospel of some modern-day evangelicals, this belief has a damaging flip side. If one believes that fertility is a sign of God's approval, then the clear implication is that *in*fertility must surely be a sign of God's *dis*pleasure — and a sure indicator of a woman's (always the woman's) unfaithfulness. Sadly, that harmful message has been conveyed across the generations in overt and covert ways, and it still sneaks into our contemporary church settings if we aren't intentional about untying that particular knot of bad theology.

Science and, to some extent, theology have evolved enough for us to know that pregnancy and childbirth are natural processes, subject to all the complications of life itself. Life, in all its forms, is certainly a gift from God. But that doesn't mean that a couple's struggle with infertility reflects God's judgment on their life. Such a shallow view of divine activity in the world negates the very premise of a compassionate and life-giving God. Furthermore, it presents a logical fallacy. Do we really believe that only "good" and deserving people become parents? Only those who will love and nurture their children and protect them from harm? We wish that would be true, but a quick glance at the headlines on any given day will sadly prove otherwise.

Such harmful theology, filled with judgment and shame, has its source not in the voice of God or angels but in the voice of humans. Namely, humans talking too much.

This story offers, among other things, a sacred invitation to hold some complicated and opposing truths together. Think of holding them in opposite hands so that you can weigh them thoughtfully, carefully, and then choose which one to keep.

On the one hand, it is true that many of our biblical stories have elements that don't hold up today, given what we know about science and the natural world, and that these stories have also been interpreted in ways that do harm, particularly to women. At the same time, in that other hand, there are also magnificent truths about God's life-giving love at work in this story! Namely, that the divine word actively steps into the world to deliver amazing news. God's activity among humans will continue in new, surprising, and miraculous ways. In God, the impossible has been made possible; there will be life where human eyes would never expect to witness it.

If this impossible birth is to be a reality, then what other impossible things might be made manifest with God?

Taking "God's favor" in the form of pregnancy out of the mix, the story of this unlikely conception contains an element of surprise—and holy terror!—that bears significant spiritual implications and an important theme of the biblical narrative. Given the fact that this is such incredibly good news, now we have to wonder—why is Zechariah so terrified when the angel of the Lord appears to him?

A High-Risk Venture

Beyond the shock factor of spotting an otherworldly being in the middle of your workplace, we might assume that Zechariah also senses the terrifying certainty that his life is about to change in a big way. And isn't change the most terrifying thing of all?

Gabriel's reassuring "don't be afraid" is followed by the news of the baby, as if having a baby is not terrifying in and of itself! Talk about facing the unknown and unknowable. Nothing will rock your ordinary world like bringing a child into it. And certainly the age factor for Zechariah and Elizabeth further complicates matters. This is a high-risk pregnancy in every possible way.

Not only is there a baby coming (surprise!) to a couple that thought that season of life was long gone (surprise again!), but this is not just any baby that's on the way. This child will be known as John the Baptizer. That name could mean bad news for his middle school years, but he'll survive that particular hazard. Still, this baby is not showing up for an ordinary life.

John the Baptizer is coming to prepare the way for another.

The son who is coming to this unlikely family will be a trailblazer. He will be a wilderness wanderer. He will speak truth to power and call out the sins of the powerful. He is going to bring a hopeful word of justice and equality that will not be met kindly by those in charge. It's the dangerous work of making a way where there is no way—in short, the work of ushering in the kingdom of heaven and making a place in the world for his cousin, Jesus.

To recap: Zechariah encounters a heavenly being in the midst of his ordinary tasks. Terrifying!

He receives impossible news, which he is simultaneously afraid to believe (it's too good to be true!) and is also afraid *might* be true (we are too old for this, Lord). He's not only going to be a father; he is going to father the resistance. He'll join the ranks of parents everywhere whose children are peacemakers and justice seekers, first responders and teachers, humanitarian aid workers and career truth tellers: in other words, this man will never sleep again.

What does he have to fear? *Literally everything.*

But what does the angel say? Do not be afraid.

Not "it will probably be okay." No platitudes or empty promises. Just a simple, impossible commandment: do not fear.

The word *angel* means, simply, "messenger." In ancient Hebrew Scriptures, an angel becomes totally transparent when speaking to a human, and they become the voice of God, with no identity or personality outside of that. For instance, the angel in the book of Genesis that appears to Hagar and tells her she will bear a son named Ishmael has no name. Same goes for the exodus story, when God promises that an angel will go ahead of the people and make a way for them. Consider them "Angel Number Five" in the credits, because they get no proper nouns. It is only in later texts, like the book of Daniel, when angels are given names of their own. In Daniel, Gabriel first appears, "having the appearance of a man."[2] Gabriel is perhaps the archetypal angel, and he appears in several other religious texts (including the Quran), but for all that familiarity, he is not so much a character in this divine drama as he is the semi-embodied voice of the Holy.

In such capacity, notice that this messenger of God does not try to overexplain the details of all that is to come. Instead, he casts a vision for the world and the gifts this child will bring to it. He doesn't say there will not be hard parts, painful moments, or long, sleepless nights. He just speaks a simple assurance that none of it is to be feared, because God will abide with loving faithfulness in every moment of it. God is there, even now, in the voice of the angel. These are not empty words of comfort so much as they are facts!

What if we were to hear that same sacred word spoken over our own lives, our own deepest fears, our darkest sleepless nights? Maybe we could name what it is we fear in the silence—and find our fear transformed by the certain presence of God.

Several years ago, I was sitting outside a cabin in Estes Park, where my husband and I were celebrating our fifteenth anniversary. It was dark out, and we were enjoying a fire in the fire pit on a very chilly evening. I was just thinking how lovely and peaceful the whole situation was when the world's most enormous grizzly bear came wandering through our driveway. It was so close that we could hear its heavy footsteps before we saw its silhouette in the motion spotlight from the cabin next door.

It was terrifying in its proximity. But because it was moving so slowly (I now truly know what the word *lumbering* means), my instinct was to be still and let it just pass by. I took some slow, deep breaths, trying not to make a sound, as I watched its breath hovering in the light in the cold night air. Even when it came so close I could literally smell that wild cologne that accompanies truly massive and untamed beasts, I just sat still until it passed by in peace.

We were done with the fire pit after that. If I recall, we skipped it (and the adjacent hot tub) for the rest of the trip!

I've often since wondered, though: How many more perceived dangers in our lives would just pass on by if we would only keep still?

Maybe if we sit in a quiet place, like Zechariah, we will find that courage for facing the unknown and seemingly terrifying is born in contemplation and stillness. Can we stay out of the noise before the rush of the season carries us away and think about who it is that we wait for? If we can do that with intention, we might find that much of what we fear simply dissolves in the resounding silence.

Discuss and Reflect

Find a Spotify playlist and chapter introduction videos to use during group study or private meditation at:

www.wjkbooks.com/CallingAllAngels

— Think of a time when you had to endure an uncomfortable silence. Why was it uncomfortable, and what did you learn??
— Think of a time when you experienced silence that was needed, restorative, or healing. How did you find that silence, and is it something you seek out regularly?

— Name out loud one thing that you are afraid of. What is it like to articulate that fear and share it with others?
— Traditionally, the first week of Advent is about hope. What is one thing you hope for yourself or for the world in this season? And what would it look like to act on that hope rather than act out of fear?
— Set an intention to embrace silence and stillness this week. Where will you find or how will you create that space? How might it change you?

Activity Idea for This Week

With your family, church group, or any group of friends and neighbors, go for a hike in a nearby park or nature preserve. If weather doesn't permit or if members of your group have physical limitations, watch a nature show together (maybe an episode of *Our Universe*, narrated by Morgan Freeman, or the Ken Burns documentary *National Parks: America's Best Idea*). Reflect on the role of nature in our lives, and how our relationship with the natural world has changed with the evolution of technology. Set some intentions together about reconnecting with natural spaces in your community, and talk about what the benefits will be for your health and your faith journey.

DAILY REFLECTIONS
Week 1, Day 1

As Pharaoh approached, the Israelites looked up, and there were the Egyptians, marching after them. They were terrified and cried out to the LORD. They said to Moses, "Was it because there were no graves in Egypt that you brought us to the desert to die? What have you done to us by bringing us out of Egypt? Didn't we say to you in Egypt, 'Leave us alone; let us serve the Egyptians'? It would have been better for us to serve the Egyptians than to die in the desert!"

Moses answered the people, "Do not be afraid. Stand firm and you will see the deliverance the LORD will bring you today. The Egyptians you see today you will never see again. The LORD will fight for you; you need only to be still."

—Exodus 14:10–14, NIV

Fear is a natural human response to danger. Many years of evolution serve us well when we are in a tight situation. Fight or flight instinct kicks in, and the resulting adrenaline can save our lives.

But so often, our body kicks off that fear response for something that is not life threatening at all. Biologically speaking, we sometimes fail to distinguish an angry email or a stressful workday from, say, getting chased by a bear. The pace of our lives and the state of the world leave our nerve endings fragile and frayed. That fight-or-flight situation can be triggered by the simplest things.

In such a state, it is hard to find peace within ourselves, much less peace for the world.

This passage finds the Israelites standing at a crossroads. They are at the brink of either total annihilation or complete freedom. And while they don't get an angelic visitation in this moment, they do get a word from God, by way of Moses: "Do not be afraid."

This is not just a holy, abstract "fear not." More to the point, Moses says, "The LORD will fight for you; you need only to be still" (v. 14, NIV).

When was the last time you faced down fear or anxiety by being still?

Remember how God protected the people of Israel as they escaped Pharoah, and how God continues to promise protection and safety now. The next time you feel the adrenaline rush that comes from anger, stress, or uncertainty, pause and take a breath. Hear the voice that speaks peace over the waters, that assures the troubled, and that casts out all fear: "The LORD will fight for you; . . . be still."

God of the desert places, we trust that you have not abandoned us to our fears. Give us wisdom to trust our instincts and discernment to know real danger from our own anxious spirit. Speak peace to our racing hearts and busy minds. Teach us to be still, trusting in your abiding presence and love. Amen.

Week 1, Day 2

There is not much use talking to [humans] about God and love if they are not able to listen. The ears with which one hears the message of the Gospel are hidden in [one's] heart, and these ears do not hear anything unless they are favored with a certain interior solitude and silence.

—Thomas Merton[3]

If we can make a regular discipline of seeking out those places of external silence, we are that much more equipped to cultivate the inner silence where true spiritual growth becomes possible.

As Thomas Merton indicates, the ears are so often hidden within the heart! I think about the noise-canceling headphones that my teenagers wear for most of the day (and, OK, that I quite often have in my own ears), and then I think: How many other vices and devices do we have that prevent us from truly hearing with our whole heart? How many distractions, diversions, and means of escapism have we cultivated, in fact, *so that* we don't have to hear all that is happening around us?

When the news is too much to bear, for instance, we can click over to another site or app that offers us only comfort and manufactured joy. The soothing aesthetics of Instagram influencers, the novel diversions of TikTok, any number of fantasy sports leagues, and, of course, pop-up ads that remind us *we should be shopping for something right now.* This is especially true in December!

We easily shift over to these venues for levity when the world has us feeling fearful. But if we could truly create the kind of space that Merton envisions, a place where we could effectively hear with our hearts a word from the holy, then we would find that we have nothing to fear from the world. Just as the world cannot meet all our deepest hopes and desires, the world also can't take away the hope that dwells in God alone.

Challenge yourself to a media fast today (or maybe even for the whole week) and see what kind of space opens up; see if you are better able to hear a word from the holy and if that word gives you courage to face something that has been making you anxious or worried.

Guard my ears from distraction today, Lord. I will set my intention to hear a word from you, a word that speaks to an inner place, even if that means hitting mute on the rest of the world for a time. Guide me in finding and keeping silence, creating a space to better hear with the heart's ears, and finding my hope in you. Speak the truth I need to hear, and make me ready to hear it. Amen.

Week 1, Day 3

The LORD is my light and my salvation—
  whom shall I fear?
The LORD is the stronghold of my life—
  of whom shall I be afraid?

When the wicked advance against me
  to devour me,
it is my enemies and my foes
  who will stumble and fall.
Though an army besiege me,
  my heart will not fear;
though war break out against me,
  even then I will be confident.

One thing I ask from the LORD,
  this only do I seek:
that I may dwell in the house of the LORD
  all the days of my life,
to gaze on the beauty of the LORD
  and to seek him in his temple.
For in the day of trouble
  he will keep me safe in his dwelling;
he will hide me in the shelter of his sacred tent
  and set me high upon a rock.
. . . .
I remain confident of this:
  I will see the goodness of the LORD
  in the land of the living.
Wait for the LORD;
  be strong and take heart
  and wait for the LORD.

                —Psalm 27:1–5, 13–14, NIV

Psalm 27 is one of my favorite passages of Scripture. Although it doesn't appear in the traditional Advent canon, it exudes all the hope and courage that the angels speak to those awaiting the birth of Christ.

Sometimes poetry and song capture what prose can't. This particular psalm is an example of how language and imagery can transcend mortal speech and paint a picture of some higher consciousness. To be confident even as the enemy advances? To sing of shelter and protection even though an army is coming at you? These are the goals of faith, to offer not just comfort but active, abiding hope, in all things.

Though not all of us living today have had the experience of facing down a literal advancing army, we certainly face any number of adversaries on a given day. In fact, the sheer number of perils that the world presents right now might seem to banish the hopefulness of these verses into oblivion. After all, what did some ancient liturgist know about mass shooters, melting ice caps, or global pandemics?

But those realities are exactly why we still need to reach for the Psalms. Ancient though they may be, there is also something timeless and timely about the absurd courage they speak in the face of peril. Whom shall we fear, indeed? Regardless of the timeframe in which they were written, the Psalms capture the full range of human experience and hardship—and offer words of hope and courage in response.

Spend some time with the Psalms in the coming weeks or early in the new year. Choose a few that speak deeply to your own experience, your own fears, your own hope for the world. Carry them with you, like a night-light through the long days of winter.

Lord, light the way for us when the road ahead seems fearful. Give us courage in the face of danger or anxiety, and lift us up to hold the light for another. We have faith that we will witness your goodness in this lifetime, in the land of the living. May it be so. Amen.

Week 1, Day 4

"But you, Bethlehem Ephrathah,
   though you are small among the clans of Judah,
out of you will come for me
   one who will be ruler over Israel,
whose origins are from of old,
   from ancient times."

Micah 5:2, NIV

Not long before Christmas, a pastor named Phillips Brooks—feeling inspired by a recent trip to the birthplace of Jesus—wrote some song lyrics and asked his church organist to compose some music to accompany them. If it came together, the song would be used for the upcoming children's Sunday school pageant.

The program, of course, was to be presented the following Sunday. As in "I need you to get this together for *this Sunday*, no pressure." (This would not be the first time in history that a pastor asked their church musician to pull something together at the last minute, especially in the run-up to Christmas time.)

By the night before the program, the organist, whose name was Louis Redner, had still not come up with the tune. But then, he says, "I was roused from sleep late in the night hearing an angel-strain whispering in my ear, and seizing a piece of music paper I jotted down the treble of the tune as we now have it, and on Sunday morning before going to church I filled in the harmony. Neither Mr. Brooks nor I ever thought the carol or the music to it would live beyond that Christmas of 1868."[4]

Turns out, it did. We now know it as "O Little Town of Bethlehem." And in the years since its birth, the beloved hymn has been recorded by Nat King Cole, Frank Sinatra, Emmylou Harris (hers is my personal favorite rendition; see the playlist that accompanies this book), and Pentatonix. Just to name a few!

We can credit Reverend Brooks and his travel-inspired lyrics for the song's lasting popularity, but it seems the real applause goes to the church musician and his receptiveness to an angel's late-night visit. 'Tis the season, after all. Lest we doubt that angels show up for us in post-biblical times, any number of authors, artists, and musicians (and maybe even preachers) will attest that their inspiration often comes from an outside—possibly even divine—source.

For my money, the power of this particular hymn comes in that iconic line: "The hopes and fears of all the years are met in thee tonight." Hope and fear are not things that many would automatically pair together like chips and queso. Hope and love, maybe. Hope and joy, of course! But hope and fear?

Of course, they are two sides of the same coin (or two sides of the same Hallmark card, if you prefer). In times of trouble or doubt, the hope side of the card is where we find our best possible outcome; then on the other side is the stuff that keeps us up nights, the worst possible scenarios that spin out in our minds and then into oblivion, that sometimes even become self-fulfilling prophecies if we aren't careful.

But hope and fear converge to form an intersection, a crossing that is in fact the perfect birthplace for God with us. Here is a great opportunity for humans to seek the divine will and presence, in the midst of our extremes, our chaos, our frequent human failing, to create the kingdom of heaven on earth. Where hope and fear meet and God steps down, hope wins the day. And we can sing about that forever.

God, give us the courage to stand in the thin and holy places where hope and fear meet. Thank you for giving us wisdom, courage, and the support of community so that we can face our fears with hope. Send us your angels when we lack inspiration, and let your creative word come live among us in new and surprising ways. Amen.

Week 1, Day 5

"Blessed be the Lord God of Israel,
   for he has looked favorably on his people
      and redeemed them.
He has raised up a mighty savior for us
   in the house of his child David,
as he spoke through the mouth of his holy
      prophets from of old,
   that we would be saved from our enemies
      and from the hand of all who hate us.
Thus he has shown the mercy promised to our
   ancestors
   and has remembered his holy covenant,
the oath that he swore to our ancestor Abraham,
   to grant us that we, being rescued from the hands
      of our enemies,
   might serve him without fear, in holiness and
      righteousness
   in his presence all our days.
And you, child, will be called the prophet of the
      Most High,
   for you will go before the Lord to prepare
      his ways."

—Luke 1:68–76

When Zechariah emerged from his long season of silence, he had a song of praise ready to lift at the birth of his son. This is a weirdly specific song to sing about a baby (recap: the baby is John the Baptist) who has literally just been born. It's quite a résumé for an infant! Granted, any proud father wants to believe that his new son will go out and do great things, maybe even changing the world. In this case, the father is not entirely wrong. As the angel Gabriel hinted to him months earlier (before the great silence), Zechariah's son will, in fact, play a big role in preparing the way for the savior of the world.

Zechariah gives praise to the God who makes all of this possible, the Holy One who will enable us to "serve him without fear" (v. 74). So this is not just a prayer about what his son, John, will do; it's not even a song about what God has done and is doing. This is a prophetic reminder that God's people have their own part to play in the still unfolding epic novel of God's activity in creation; we are to serve *without fear.* And in spite of everything, God has made a way where there is no way and continues to empower us with the courage to do likewise.

So let's ask ourselves again, what would we do if we weren't afraid?

God of hope, we live our own hope each day, trusting that your promises transcend all our human fears. Send your empowering spirit to guide and lift us when we need it most so that we can love and serve, wonderfully, miraculously unafraid. Amen.

SECOND WEEK OF ADVENT

Call and Response

I t was finally my turn.

I was nine years old. And, having played an angel or a sheep in every church Christmas pageant in my young memory, *this year I was going to be Mary.*

Just to be clear, it was no dazzling talent or captivating stage presence that won me the role. It was the fact that I had a baby brother who was the perfect age to be Jesus that year. When the time came for him to be "born," they set him down in the aisle, wearing a shining halo of Christmas tree tinsel around his one-year-old head. I held out my arms, and he crawled down the aisle to me and took his place in the stable. The scene was complete, even if this Jesus was a bit too big to be lying in a manger and nearly ready to run off and preach in the temple; we had effectively told the story of Christmas that everyone comes to church to hear.

It was adorable, don't get me wrong. So cute I didn't even mind being upstaged in my main character moment. My main character moment that came with *zero speaking part*. Because in that part of the Gospel story, Mary doesn't say much. She holds things in her heart, silently.

The irony of the silent role of Mary in many of our church nativity plays is that the actual Mary of Scripture has quite a lot to say. More, in fact, than any other woman in the biblical narrative; even more than any other woman in Luke[1]—which is saying something, as Luke's is the only Gospel in which women speak at all. But Mary's speaking role does not actually occur on the mainstage of Christmas Eve. It happens approximately nine months before, when she receives some terrifying news. Before we get to Mary's revolutionary not-so-silent monologue, though, let's start with another angelic encounter.

Mary's Angel

In the sixth month the angel Gabriel was sent by God to a town in Galilee called Nazareth, to a virgin engaged to a man whose name was Joseph, of the house of David. The virgin's name was Mary. And he came to her and said, "Greetings, favored one! The Lord is with you." But she was much perplexed by his words and pondered what sort of greeting this might be. The angel said to her, "Do not be afraid, Mary, for you have found favor with God. And now, you will conceive in your womb and bear a son, and you will name him Jesus. He will be great and will be called the Son of the Most High, and the Lord God will give to him the throne of his ancestor David. He will reign over the house of Jacob forever, and of his kingdom there will be no end." Mary said to the angel, "How can this be, since I am a virgin?" The angel said to her, "The Holy Spirit will come upon you, and the power of the Most High will overshadow you; therefore the child to be born will be holy; he will be called Son of God. And now, your relative Elizabeth in her old age has also conceived a son, and this is the sixth month for her who was said to be barren. For nothing will be impossible with God." Then Mary said, "Here am I, the servant of the Lord; let it be with me according to your word." Then the angel departed from her.

—Luke 1:26–38

If you're getting Zechariah vibes here, it's not a coincidence. The story unfolds in a familiar pattern: like the priest before her (who happens to be married to her beloved cousin, Elizabeth), Mary is going about her regular, everyday life. At this point, that ordinary life involves wedding plans for the near future, as she is betrothed to Joseph. Minding her own business, she, too, encounters an angel. Much like Zechariah, her immediate response is holy terror!

And, much like Zechariah, Mary has big questions. Here is another perplexed recipient of unbelievable news; another pregnancy that is, to say the least, biologically impossible! At this point, she remains "unmarried" in the most critical way. You can't blame a girl for being skeptical.

This is where the similarities between the two stories and situations start to diverge a bit. Zechariah is a man; he is of age, he is married, and as a priest, he holds a great deal of privilege and authority. Mary, on the other hand, is a quadruple whammy of young, unmarried, poor, and female. And now she's supposed to add *pregnant* to that résumé.

What does she have to fear? *Literally everything.*

But what does the angel say? *Do not be afraid.*

That part, too, echoes the angel's visit with Zechariah. But in this case, those instructions seem like a much taller order. She is to bear the son of the living God without having known intimacy with her husband. You know the neighbors are going to talk.

It's one thing to "not be afraid" when you are in a position of privilege and people will believe, listen to, and respect you; when your life is not in danger, when your body is not vulnerable to both physical abuse and the trials of pregnancy. It's another thing entirely when there are any number of perils between you and the delivery date.

But the angel has assured her that the Lord is with her. And that, for her, seems to be enough.

This is not just a story about an angel's visit to a young girl. This is a life-changing call and response. And respond Mary does. She goes to her cousin, Elizabeth (who, recap, is also pregnant!), and she shares her good news in song:

And Mary said,

"My soul magnifies the Lord,
    and my spirit rejoices in God my Savior,
for he has looked with favor on the lowly state of
    his servant.
    Surely from now on all generations will
      call me blessed,
for the Mighty One has done great things for me,
    and holy is his name;
indeed, his mercy is for those who fear him
    from generation to generation.
He has shown strength with his arm;
    he has scattered the proud in the imagination
      of their hearts.
He has brought down the powerful from their
      thrones
    and lifted up the lowly;
he has filled the hungry with good things
    and sent the rich away empty.
He has come to the aid of his child Israel,
    in remembrance of his mercy,
according to the promise he made to our ancestors,
    to Abraham and to his descendants forever."

—Luke 1:46–55

This is the part we tend to omit from our church Christmas pageants. We skip over to the Linus moment, where "there were . . . shepherds abiding in the field" (2:8, KJV). But Mary's song is truly the word that the church and the world need to hear, maybe now more than ever.

Whereas the pronouncement to Zechariah was followed by a long silence, Mary's response comes immediately. She's got a long wait ahead of her, to be sure. Her wilderness season will present its own trials. But she is quite vocal about what all this means for her and what it will mean for the weary world.

Isn't it interesting, how the longest stretch of Scripture in a woman's voice happens in the same Gospel, even the same chapter, where a man has been, somehow, divinely silenced?

The great reordering that Mary sings about here has already begun.[2] Let the lowly be lifted up. Let the silent speak and be heard.

Let the weak and oppressed be finally unafraid.

A song like that can only be called "Magnificat." A hymn of praise to the Lord.

As much as I love a good "marketable" church Christmas pageant, and as a pastor I have put one together myself a time or two, the world is waiting for the Mary who sings prophetic wisdom and shouts her praise, not the one who takes a reflective, submissive posture in the manger scene. Mary, pure and lowly. Mary, meek and mild . . . she appears for the grand finale, not a hair out of place after giving birth in a barn (with no drugs!), settling into the manger scene just in time to sing "Silent Night."

Is that supposed to be the same girl who sings about sending the rich away empty and *throwing* the mighty from their thrones? Bring her back. We need her.

Many artists throughout history have rendered images of Mary standing on a serpent (a reference to Genesis 3:15). As contemporary renderings go, I really love artist Ben Wildflower's version. In his artwork, Mary is not sitting quietly. This Mary stands tall. Her fist is raised in protest, and her foot is crushing the head of a snake. The words of the Magnificat encircle the image.[3]

We need to hear more from that kind of Mary. We need that Mary who's trampling injustice with her bare feet! We need to let her sing more. Because that Mary sounds like a woman

who will raise a son
who will turn over the tables of money changers
    in the temple,
who will have dinner with tax collectors and
    prostitutes,
who will insist that people stop throwing stones,
    and intercede for the children,
who will preach up such a storm about bringing
    hope to the poor and justice to the oppressed
that people might just get uncomfortable
    enough… to want to kill him.

Nothing to Fear but Fear Itself

Two thousand years later, our world finds itself ravaged by greed. The powerful have effectively destroyed the earth that we call home; the gap between rich and poor grows as billionaires buy political power and the poor and vulnerable feel the most dramatic impacts of climate change. Racial inequality persists, as does mainstream refusal to reckon with it in any meaningful way. Mass incarceration is a widely acceptable (and legal—see the Thirteenth Amendment) form of slavery. Women remain woefully underrepresented in the highest seats of power in most every developed nation in the world. Children die at the U.S. border as politicians run on platforms of American nationalism, pledging again to keep "those people" out for another four years.

Every one of these human crises is created by the voices of human fear. These outcomes are the small, sour fruits of fearful living and represent the antithesis of the kingdom of heaven. A disproportionate weight of human suffering is, in fact, created by those who hold power and desire only to maintain their power at any human cost. This perpetuates cycles of fear that ripple throughout our world. Powerful people commit atrocities out of their own fear and insecurity. Those who suffer at their hands then live in fear of the next wave of terror.

Those who witness unjust realities become fearful as well: What will be the consequences if we intervene? In the face of both overt and covert oppression, people of privilege are often concerned but not concerned enough to risk losing their privilege. Martin Luther King Jr. spoke to this dynamic when he said:

> I must confess that over the last few years I have been gravely disappointed with the white moderate. I have almost reached the regrettable conclusion that the Negro's great stumbling block in the stride toward freedom is not the White Citizen's Counciler or the Ku Klux Klanner, but the white moderate who is more devoted to "order" than to justice; who prefers a negative peace which is the absence of tension to a positive peace which is the presence of justice; who constantly says "I agree with you in the goal you seek, but I can't agree with your methods of direct action;" who paternalistically feels he can set the timetable for another man's freedom; who

lives by the myth of time and who constantly advises the Negro to wait until a "more convenient season."[4]

The widespread desire for such negative peace, or passive peace, stems from a deeply rooted fear of disruption in our collective psyche. So pervasive is the fear of unsettling the perceived order that even those who claim to desire the unsettling peace of Christ for the world take active part in maintaining the status quo of inequality. Our unbalanced systems are like a weighted blanket that provides comfort while also limiting our mobility for change. It is imperative for the good of all that those in positions of privilege climb out from under that blanket and join the work of positive peace. After years of accepting that a degree of white supremacy is inevitable in our communities, finding the courage to accept the harm we've been a part of perpetuating—and then getting busy to change it—is a terrifying prospect.

But what will happen if we don't?

At times, contemplative silence can be an essential part of our spiritual journey as well as a practice at the heart of social change. But passive silence in the face of injustice works in direct opposition to true justice and peace. Isabel Wilkerson addresses the evil of silence in *Caste: The Origins of Our Discontent*. This timely and powerful book addresses the roots of our inherent social structures in America and works to unwind some of the history and ongoing contributing factors that keep us bound by this system. She notes how those with power in the caste system were content to stand by and watch atrocities like lynching take place in their community, "as long as people accepted them and gained a sense of order and means of justification for the cruelties to which they had grown accustomed, inequalities that they took to be the laws of nature."[5] Wilkerson's examination of our national identity is required reading for those who truly wish to embrace the kind of positive peace that Mary sang about, the kind of peace we claim to await in this Advent season.

The story of Advent is not meant to be a solo or even just an angelic chorus. It is a call and response. The angels say "do not be afraid," and the faithful are compelled to answer back. In fact, it is the very essence of our life's work to determine how we will respond: Will we locate our own voices among the fearful, trying to hold onto power and whatever privilege we can grasp? Or will we answer the angel's call with courageous responses and answer the world's voices of fear by witnessing to courageous peace and radical justice?

In the neighborhood where my church lives and serves, a blacksmith named Craig works with local gun violence prevention groups. Together they collect guns that have either been seized by law enforcement or given up willingly by their owners, and then Craig forges the weapons into garden tools. His work is part of a "guns to gardens" project in partnership with several local churches, inspired by Isaiah 2:4: "They shall beat their swords into plowshares and their spears into pruning hooks."

Before Jesus was born, Mary had a bold vision of a world utterly transformed. Turning guns into gardening tools is just one small glimpse of how people give voice to that song again, welcoming a child who will be Prince of Peace, not a god of war.

The angels still call, "Do not be afraid." How will the faithful respond?

What if we learned to sing the Magnificat, knowing it by heart as well as "Silent Night"?

What would we do if we weren't afraid?

Discuss and Reflect

Find a Spotify playlist and chapter introduction videos to use during group study or private meditation at:

www.wjkbooks.com/CallingAllAngels

— What do you remember about how the Christmas story was portrayed to you as a child? If you never learned the Christmas story in church, what parts of the narrative did you pick up elsewhere?
— Can you think of a courageous woman in your life who defied the limitations that her role in society might have placed on her? What did you learn from her?
— How can we use our own voices and places of privilege to speak for the poor and the oppressed?
— What common human fears do you think have the most harmful effects on humanity? And how can the Gospel speak peace to those fears and bring about justice?
— In what situations do you notice yourself or others settling for what King called "a negative

peace which is the absence of tension [rather than] a positive peace which is the presence of justice"? What would that positive peace look like in our world?

Activity Idea for This Week

With your family, church group, or any group of friends and neighbors, find a local holiday concert, play, or church program to attend together. This can be anything from your city's symphony and chorale performance of Handel's *Messiah* to a kids' holiday program at a local elementary school. Most communities will have a range of offerings falling somewhere in between. If you can't find anything that works for your group, stream and watch a favorite Christmas movie or concert together. (Add some popcorn and hot chocolate and make it a watch party!) Focus on how the story or even just the message of the Christmas season is portrayed in your chosen performance. Where does it echo the biblical Christmas story, and where is the message different? Does it offer a perspective or voice that helps bring the story into the present day? Whose voice is missing?

DAILY REFLECTIONS

Week 2, Day 1

Then Hannah prayed and said:
  "My heart rejoices in the LORD;
    in the LORD my horn is lifted high.
  My mouth boasts over my enemies,
    for I delight in your deliverance.

  "There is no one holy like the LORD;
    there is no one besides you;
    there is no Rock like our God.

  "Do not keep talking so proudly
    or let your mouth speak such arrogance,
  for the LORD is a God who knows,
    and by him deeds are weighed.

  "The bows of the warriors are broken
    but those who stumbled are armed with
      strength.
  Those who were full hire themselves out for food,
    but those who were hungry are hungry no
      more."

— 1 Samuel 2:1–5a, NIV

Does this sound familiar?

It is the song Hannah sings as she gives her son over to the Lord. Like Elizabeth after her — and like Sarah before them both — Hannah prays for a child for a long time before God gives her a son. Now, when he is still young, Hannah takes the child to the temple, along with an offering, and sings her praise to the Lord. She offers up his gifts for service to the Lord, just as she received the child as a gift from God.

The themes of Hannah's song sound very much like Mary's. She envisions God working through her son for a great reordering of the world. It is a world in which the weak become strong, weapons are destroyed, and the hungry are fed.

This passage serves as a great reminder that certain themes echo throughout Scripture, as God's creative work continues to unfold through human belief and activity. Notice how it is often women's voices who speak the language of revolutionary nonviolence—perhaps because women have historically not held military or political power in mainstream institutions. Their place in God's story, then, is to draw attention to the very structures that the arc of salvation will bend and transform.

Those themes of nonviolence, care for the poor, and the upheaval of worldly power structures turn out to be the overarching themes of Jesus' life and ministry as well. Throughout the Gospel story, and in particular the Gospel of Luke, those with the least power are the ones who give voice to the powerful transformation taking place through the teaching, healing, and miraculous acts of Jesus.

Let the songs of these and other women of our faith story call our attention to the voices we need to pay most attention to in our present context. Who are the unheard and the unseen whom God would have us lift up? Who is singing a song of revolutionary nonviolence and a love that will turn the world's wealth and war machines upside down? Who is calling us to be unafraid?

Unsettling God, thank you for prophetic women in our past and in our midst. May we learn from them what it is to speak with courage. May we listen to those voices that often go unheard but that bear living witness to the power of your Spirit. Amen.

Week 2, Day 2

The world would be a paradise of peace and justice if global citizens shared a common definition of love which would guide our thoughts and action.

—bell hooks[6]

Fear is born from ignorance. We think that the other person is trying to take away something from us. But if we look deeply, we see that the desire of the other person is exactly our own desire—to have peace, to be able to have a chance to live. . . . The only answer to fear is more understanding.

—Thich Nhat Hanh[7]

On the surface, what could legendary author and activist bell hooks—a lifelong Kentuckian—and Vietnamese Buddhist monk Thich Nhat Hanh possibly have in common?

Both were poets, visionaries, and spiritual guides to many. And they shared a radical vision of the peace that is possible in the world, not in some far-off sense, but in the right now, if humans could latch on to what we share and not what divides us. The two shared an unlikely kinship through their work and philosophies and, strangely enough, died within just a few weeks of each other (hooks in December of 2021 and Hanh in January of 2022). But they each left a legacy of treasured verse and prose that enters the canon of modern-day prophets.

The quotes above are from a conversation hooks transcribed that is well worth your time, during Advent or any season.

As Hanh states, "fear is born from ignorance." And as we well know, violence is so often born of fear. The best hope for our violent, warring world, then, is deep knowledge — not in the bookish sense but in the human sense: knowledge of another's experience, compassion for another's journey, empathy for another's pain. If God's people were to make that kind of deep knowing the goal of our living, then we could live God's kingdom into reality in our time. As hooks said, "the world would be a paradise of peace and justice."

How might you contribute to that kind of compassionate knowing today?

Lord, you have searched us and known us in our inner being. Give us the vision and holy wisdom that we might seek to know others as you know us: that strangers might become beloveds and that the world might see an end to violence and fear.

Week 2, Day 3

Maybe not in time for you and me
But someday at Christmastime.

—Stevie Wonder[8]

Unlike Wham!'s "Last Christmas," Stevie Wonder sings of next Christmas. Or the next. Or perhaps the one after that . . .

His is a vision of "someday" and all that it implies. A dream of world peace, where no one is hungry, where love prevails, and where "no man has fears."[9] It sounds a lot like the Magnificat, doesn't it?

In the great future someday, perhaps things are possible that are not immediately within our grasp. Someday is a wide-open space full of hope and possibility. It provides space for dreaming.

At some point in the days of the early church, the faithful started to realize that Jesus' return was not, perhaps, as imminent as they thought. Maybe they were going to be at this healing and feeding work for a while. Maybe he wasn't even going to show back up in their lifetime. But they continued to go around, sharing the good news and sharing stories of resurrection, in the hope of a great someday. It was a season of planting seeds for a future they might not live to see but believed in and longed for nonetheless.

Let the season of Advent be a seed-planting time—when God's people go about the work of sowing the beginnings of the world we long for, which reveals the kingdom of God in our midst.

Maybe not in time for you and me, but someday at Christmas time . . .

God of the great someday, our hope is in the future you have promised and in the love we witness here, among us now. Give us the courage to plant seeds for that future and to bear witness to its goodness right now. Amen.

Week 2, Day 4

"But you, Israel, my servant,
  Jacob, whom I have chosen,
  you descendants of Abraham my friend,
I took you from the ends of the earth,
  from its farthest corners I called you.
I said, 'You are my servant';
  I have chosen you and have not rejected you.
So do not fear, for I am with you;
  do not be dismayed, for I am your God.
I will strengthen you and help you;
  I will uphold you with my righteous right hand."
  —Isaiah 41:8–10, NIV

Throughout the stories and prophetic texts of the Old Testament, the people of Israel move in and out of faithfulness to their covenant with God. There are times when they are living their best lives, following all the commandments and being the chosen people with dignity. Then there are the other times . . .

Most of us can relate to that kind of faith journey, can we not? There are days when it all makes sense, when we feel God's presence with us as certainly as an angel on our shoulder. Days when we are living at the intersection of who we believe God to be and how we are called to serve the world with our best gifts. Days when we are guided by grace and wisdom, knowing that we are blessed and beloved, and we can give our love freely to others.

Then there are the other times . . .

If we are human people, there are also going to be days when our doubts are bigger than our faith. When we stumble and fall short of extending the grace we have received. When we act out our worst impulses, worship the idols of wealth and status, and watch TikTok videos until our eyeballs freeze open rather than sharing in fellowship with our neighbors.

That is part of the journey.

This is how it has always been. People wander in and out of faithfulness and good behavior. And while the goal should always be to err on the side of faith and discipline, the prophets remind us that, even in those times when God's people wandered away from the path, God never abandoned them. God spoke words of assurance again and again: that there was nothing to fear, that they had the strength of the almighty behind them, and that help was on the way.

Almighty one, forgive us when we wander from your will, when we fall short of answering your call on our lives and living faithfully your commandments. Set us on the right path again, with no fear of retribution but only the certainty of your abiding love. Amen.

Week 2, Day 5

Peace I leave with you; my peace I give you. I
do not give to you as the world gives. Do not let
your hearts be troubled and do not be afraid.
                                    —John 14:27, NIV

From the angels that spoke to his mother before
he was born, Jesus perhaps picked up a sacred
word to be delivered at a precise moment. Because
it just so happened that, in a moment when Jesus
was saying goodbye to those he loved the most—in
a moment when he had everything to fear and so
did they, by proximity—he repeated the familiar
refrain: *do not be afraid*.

These were unsettling times. Danger and threats
of violence were everywhere. Jesus knew that his
time on earth was short, and he tried to prepare the
disciples, who would continue the work of healing,
teaching, and feeding folks after he was gone.

He alludes to resurrection and to the place he will
prepare for them in his father's house. He speaks
words of courage and assurance. But he does not
promise them that the world will be perfect or even
kind. He leaves them with a different kind of peace,
not "as the world gives," but one that can come only
from someplace divine.

This is the kind of peace that Jesus taught all his
life and in fact lived by his way of dying. It isn't a
peace that comes from absence of conflict but a way
of life that God's people choose, with intention, in
spite of the world's seeming unwillingness to come
along with us.

It is a trail that the faithful must blaze in wilderness places and in the middle of crowded city streets. It is the way of John the Baptist, the way of Mary's song, and the way that Jesus calls us to still. The work of Advent is to make a way where there is no way, with the courage of angels and the model of Jesus to guide us.

Holy Wisdom, set us on the path of peace — not peace as the world promises but the peace that only you can bring. Let us be instruments of your peace in this season, and all the days that we're living. We seek you in the name of Jesus, who showed us the way of the blessed peacemakers. Amen.

THIRD WEEK
OF ADVENT

The Hopes and Fears of All the Years

Mary has received the life-changing news that she will mother the Son of God. Her response is first shock, then fear, then deep skepticism, and then finally not just acceptance but a powerful, prophetic response to this call of the divine. She sings of government machines disabled, systems of oppression dismantled, the hungry fed, and justice extended to all. Then she goes to visit her cousin where they have a lovely pregnant ladies' retreat while also plotting the resistance and dreaming of how their sons shall one day usher in the kingdom of God.

Meanwhile . . . a carpenter named Joseph is about to get the shock of his life.

Matthew is the only Gospel that tells Joseph's side of the story. Each Gospel writer had their reasons for sharing the perspective that they did. Because Matthew's author wrote for a primarily Jewish audience, it would have been important to establish Jesus as a homeboy with a righteous Jewish father. It lends credibility (he's from a good family! he's one of us!) with Matthew's particular reading circle. This Gospel telling also places Jesus' lineage within the house of David, giving him the authority of both a royal heritage and another strong point of identity and connection to the people of Israel.

But while Matthew's Gospel seems to come from a specifically Jewish point of view, it is also the Gospel most critical of some Jewish customs and traditions, particularly of those at the top of the religious hierarchy, the scribes and the Pharisees.[1] Some Christian leaders throughout history have misused such texts as a basis and defense for anti-Jewish sentiment. But on the contrary, Matthew's critique of those who misused their power within the religious system shows a certain respect for the system—much like contemporary Christians who struggle with some of the church's historically wrong-sided teachings but remain part of the faith and seek to make its institutions more just. Matthew's Gospel demonstrates that there is a way to be faithful to God while also challenging the institutions in which humans try to contain God!

In Matthew's Gospel, there is a place for tradition. But there is also a time and a place for letting go of ancient law and custom and discerning what new thing God might be doing in the present moment. The story of Jesus' birth to the world might have gone a lot differently if this carpenter named Joseph had been a man more bound by tradition.

Joseph's Angel

This is how the birth of Jesus the Messiah came about: His mother Mary was pledged to be married to Joseph, but before they came together, she was found to be pregnant through the Holy Spirit. Because Joseph her husband was faithful to the law, and yet did not want to expose her to public disgrace, he had in mind to divorce her quietly.

But after he had considered this, an angel of the Lord appeared to him in a dream and said, "Joseph son of David, do not be afraid to take Mary home as your wife, because what is conceived in her is from the Holy Spirit. She will give birth to a son, and you are to give him the name Jesus, because he will save his people from their sins."

All this took place to fulfill what the Lord had said through the prophet: "The virgin will conceive and give birth to a son, and they will call him Immanuel" (which means "God with us").

When Joseph woke up, he did what the angel of the Lord had commanded him and took Mary home as his wife. But he did not consummate their marriage until she gave birth to a son. And he gave him the name Jesus.

—Matthew 1:18–25, NIV

Joseph finds himself in a devastating predicament. These verses give us a glimpse into the scandal. Here is the tabloid, real-time rendition of what happens when the activity of an other-worldly God crosses into the realm of mortals.

In first-century Jewish life, in Mary and Joseph's world, this kind of news does not go down well. Different translations of Scripture use different words to describe their relationship at that time: "engaged," "pledged," or "espoused." Whichever word you choose, their arrangement was not just social; by Jewish law this was a legally binding contract. They had not yet set up housekeeping together, but legally—as far as their family and community were concerned—they were married.

So Mary turning up pregnant is, let's say, awkward. Joseph knows that their marriage is not official yet in at least one critical way, and so he cannot be the father. Even nowadays, that kind of news would be grounds for calling off the whole deal. Back then, it was a crime. In Joseph's world, he has only two options available to him: One is to divorce her; the other is to submit her for public stoning, as indicated in Deuteronomic law. In this case, divorce is clearly the good-guy move! And Matthew's author even goes so far as to specify that Joseph will "divorce her quietly," revealing perhaps the depths of his compassion—even before his life-changing encounter with a divine being.

Into this moment of human confusion and upheaval, an angel appears.

The term "angel of the Lord" is worth noting. In the Jewish apocalyptic tradition, angels of the Lord bring messages from God to reveal the unfolding of God's purposes for creation—just as Joseph's angel does in this scene. Joseph's angel of the Lord is doing exactly that. And this is surely an apocalyptic moment in every sense of the word—for the world in general, and for Joseph in particular. With the birth of this child, God is doing a new thing. Nothing will be as it was. This is, of course, good news! But we can see why Joseph may not think so in the moment. If his initial response is visible fear (to which the angel is presumably responding), that is an understandable human reaction.

What the angel suggests is no small thing. The messenger essentially tells Joseph to put aside everything he knows—about culture and custom, about love and fidelity, about family and gender roles and power. It's an impossible request.

But the angel speaks: *do not be afraid*. And as we've noticed by now, those four little words can accomplish the impossible.

In telling Joseph to stay married and raise this child as his own, the angel is essentially calling Joseph to abandon all his values, to take on a wife who is carrying a child who does not, in the strictest sense, belong to him. This is not exactly a Hallmark Christmas movie we've walked into here. But whatever else may come, he awoke the morning after that angelic visit, got up, and did what the angel had told him.

That must have been some angel—some powerful, heavenly being who could speak so simply and make a righteous man forget everything he knows about the way the world is supposed to work, lay down his pride, and take on the life-changing and world-shaping role of nurturing the Son of God. Or perhaps it wasn't all up to the angel. Maybe Joseph himself possessed some brand of inner grit that allowed him to see past the anxiety of the present moment and muster the courage to move forward in faith. And, in fact, this courage is the heart of Matthew's Gospel! It's all about that fearful intersection between honoring tradition and being held captive by it; between knowing the past and believing what might be possible in the future; between what has happened in the known world and what it might yet become.

Joseph might have easily been bound by tradition. He could have said, "Thanks but no thanks" to taking Mary as his wife and her son as his son. After all, her perceived indiscretion would have brought horrible shame not only to him but to his whole family. By all appearances, Mary had committed a terrible crime against them all. Custom dictated that her apparent sin breached not just a husband's pride but property laws as well—women were considered property of their husbands, a dynamic that adds to the scandal of her perceived sin.

If Joseph had declined the angel's invitation, he would have missed his chance to be part of a miracle. While God would surely still have made another way, Joseph's hesitation in that moment would have thrown a snag in the whole plan God had set in motion. As a righteous man, Joseph could have kept looking in the rearview mirror and hanging on to his past expectations instead of taking part in God's future. And because he was considered a righteous man, no one would have blamed him in the least!

But when the angel spoke, Joseph somehow found the faith to overcome his fear. He leaned into the forward motion of the Spirit and took his place in all the amazing things that God had planned.

The Wages of Fear

Some say that money is the root of all evil. But I'd venture that fear does far more harm than money. Maybe that's why the angels announcing Jesus' birth are so quick to address human fear and take it out of the equation—because really not much else can happen as long as people are afraid and stuck. The story of the nativity doesn't have much room to move if fear rules.

And maybe that's why so much of Scripture is focused on the message to be unafraid. As long as we're bound by fear, we can't fully live into God's call on our lives or God's creative vision for the world. We do a lot of sitting still, looking back, and wishing that things were easier, less messy, and more like the good old days.

In this exceedingly anxious time in which we find ourselves living, wouldn't it be great if a heavenly host would descend and speak four words that would change everything, guiding us to let go of what we thought the world was going to be and lean into the reality of the present moment with compassion and conviction? That's the angel we need, calling us out of our fear and into action and movement. Because it sure does feel like a mess around here lately.

In the years since the COVID-19 pandemic, the world we've inherited bears little resemblance to the world we were prepared for. Things that seemed certain for past generations now seem tenuous, the literal ground we stand on unsteady beneath our feet. So many of the institutions we've always built life around failed our communities miserably during those years—from health care to childcare to education—while others have struggled to regain any semblance of normalcy in the recovery years. Communities of faith, which were already facing challenging realities regarding participation, are now fighting an uphill battle for their very existence. Many churches are still reeling from the financial hardship of those fallow years, not to mention the comfort level folks discovered with *just not going to church*. I guess tradition can't quite fix everything. (Isn't it ironic that we long for a past reality that, in the end, was not sufficient to meet our needs in a time of true crisis?)

The economic impacts of the pandemic years continue to ripple and hit us all close to home. The sticker shock at the grocery store is real—and wages haven't budged much in a couple of decades. Home ownership is creeping out of reach for the (disappearing) middle class, as is a college education. And it doesn't help at all that the political rhetoric around all of this has only gotten more toxic and convoluted in the intervening years.

This is not a doom inventory, just a short reality check. The world in which we're living now is not the world that we signed up for. It's not the one they prepared us for in high school or Sunday school. Who knows what the coming years will bring and which of our institutions will be left standing for the next generation?

In our chronic condition of being human, all that uncertainty might make us afraid.

We are apt to look around and wonder if maybe God has decided we aren't worth the trouble after all. We wonder if the whole "baby in a manger" thing has been canceled. Are we all standing here just watching an empty sky? Where is our divine intervention? That dramatic in-breaking of the Spirit that calls a weary world to put aside fear and rejoice?

The great and terrible news is this: *we might be it.* The greatest hope for that desperate and fragile place we know as the world right now might rest in our own hands and within our own collective voice.

It's scary at first when we recognize that no army is going to show up and fix it all, when we remember that the baby who's coming will bring peace rather than a forceful course correction. But then we remember: that's the good news. That the baby everyone was waiting for meant God was doing a new thing that humans had never dared to dream of before.

Notice that unlike Mary and Zechariah, Joseph doesn't have a solo ballad to sing after his angelic visit. In fact, he doesn't speak at all. His action—responding faithfully to the angel's command—becomes his part in the story.[2] Everything relies not on what he will say in that critical moment but on what he will do.

Much like Joseph, people of faith today find ourselves standing at a terrifying intersection between the world we knew and the one in which we actually live. And like Joseph, we are faced with some game-changing decisions. Do we reach backward and cling to tradition, even when it no longer serves us or meets the need of the moment? Or do we hear the timeless words of the holy messengers—*do not be afraid*—and put all our faith into the world that is still becoming?

The new thing that God, even now, might be working in our midst?

Can we hear that call to be unafraid and act accordingly?

If we speak with courage into the void, we find that angels are not always the dazzling, glittery, gold-and-white stuff of children's books and Christmas pageants but our own movement as ambassadors of God's love in the world: making Christmas happen for families in our neighborhood, taking coats to refugees and toys to foster children, singing carols for the homebound, and feeding the hungry close to home and around the world.

Writer and activist Parker Palmer calls this the work of "bringing Christmas back down to earth."[3] It is the discipline of recognizing our own responsibility to transform reality—to be peacemakers, to fight for equality, and to seek justice for the poor, even when the world remains fearful and uncertain.

When we stop being guided by fear of what we might lose if we let go of the past, God's people can be a powerful presence in impossible places.

Joy in the Morning

Let the story of Joseph's courage in an impossible moment remind us that Jesus does not come to a world where all is well; Jesus comes to a broken world in the cold of winter. And he is not born to those who are perfect and whole; he is born to the poor, the weary, the brokenhearted, and the doubtful. He comes to the world as it is—real life, messy and frayed. He comes as love incarnate, bringing peace to all who will receive it and to all who speak its birth. He brings joy to impossible places. And he leads us out of the bounds of how it's always been and into the promise of all that might be, in the becoming kingdom of God.

Discuss and Reflect

Find a Spotify playlist and chapter introduction videos to use during group study or private meditation at:

www.wjkbooks.com/CallingAllAngels

— Think of some holiday traditions that your family keeps. How did they start, and why have they lasted?
— What are some ways in which tradition can be meaningful and good? How might tradition also pose challenges?
— How would this story have been different if Joseph had bowed to societal expectations and not listened to the angel? If he had responded to his situation from a place of fear instead of a place of faith?
— What are some traditions or cultural norms that people of faith may need to overcome in order to live faithfully in this moment? How might we answer some of our present challenges with forward-looking faith rather than fear?
— How can we find and claim moments of joy in the midst of dark or difficult seasons? How does joy empower us to overcome fear?

Activity Idea for This Week

With your family, church group, or any group of friends and neighbors, take an active joy break! Make small bags of snacks and personal care items to share with unhoused neighbors or stop and visit someone who is homebound and deliver some treats to them. Try to make it to a part of town you don't usually frequent. Though weather may not permit it in your part of the world, you might even plant a tree this week, or some seasonally appropriate indoor potted plants. Maybe take one to someone who is confined to their home from your church or neighborhood. Think about how you are placing your faith in God's future by planting new life and sharing joy.

DAILY REFLECTIONS

Week 3, Day 1

A shoot will come up from the stump of Jesse;
    from his roots a Branch will bear fruit.
The Spirit of the Lord will rest on him—
    the Spirit of wisdom and of understanding,
    the Spirit of counsel and of might,
    the Spirit of the knowledge and fear of the
       Lord—
and he will delight in the fear of the Lord.
               —Isaiah 11:1–3, NIV

I used to think the house next door was cursed. We've lived in our house five years, and in that time, three different families have come and gone (we aren't terrible neighbors, I swear!). The family that's there now have been there over a year now, so they appear to be lifers.

There used to be an enormous tree in the front yard. Massive. And one of the first things this new family did when they moved in was to have it taken down. It was an ordeal. It took a professional crew with a big truck and heavy equipment several *days* to take it down. But the stump remains, and even the stump is huge—bigger than my coffee table! Not even that professional crew with their big truck and heavy equipment could get that whole thing out of there without completely unearthing the neighborhood.

If you've ever tried to pull up the stump of an old tree, you know it can be almost impossible to uproot entirely. There will always be traces of that old growth just beneath the surface.

The prophet Isaiah talked about things that would come up in their season. He referred to a certain "stump," the remnant of the line of Jesse, that would produce new growth when everyone least suspected it. This text is situated after passages dealing with injustice and Israel's years of sin and wandering away from their covenant with God, but the roots of God's people have not been entirely pulled out of the ground. God will fulfill the promise of an heir to the throne of David. The new king will lead with righteousness and mercy. The new branch of the family tree will produce a leader whose reign will bring peace and justice for all.

Whether you think Isaiah was talking about Jesus the Messiah or not (likely not), we can all relate to the hope that God will bring new growth to old and seemingly dying places.

People say that the church as we know it is dying because it doesn't look like it once did. But those who are actively involved in vital congregations—of all shapes and sizes—know otherwise. Leaders in those communities see the signs of new kinds of growth, where God is doing a new thing. Even if the mid-twentieth-century church is no longer a viable vision, the church has all new ways of connecting with local communities that would never have been possible before.

I also think about the courage that Joseph found to let go some of the laws and customs that limited his choices in a difficult moment and to trust that God might be doing something new that he wanted to see unfold.

If we trusted that God was still speaking and moving among us, we'd know that change doesn't always mean death. We'd know that even death is nothing to be feared. And if we could overcome that ultimate human fear of death, then what else could possibly scare us?

I finally told my neighbor that I had been worried about a curse on his house. "But now you're here and your family is staying," I said, "so clearly it's fine."

And he said, "I think the tree was the curse. It was sick. It was going to fall on the house. It just needed to come down."

Sometimes you have to cut away the old branches to see what the stump can do.

Sometimes you have to be unafraid of what you're losing to see what God wants to give you right now.

God, help us to see the things from the past that are holding us back, and grant us the courage to leave those things behind. Show us what miracles can come from the stumps that remain. Amen.

Week 3, Day 2

Deep in their roots, all flowers keep the light.
—Theodore Roethke[4]

Traditionally speaking, the Third Sunday of Advent is intended to be a bit of a break in what was otherwise a dark, solemn season for penitence and reflection. Otherwise known as "Gaudete Sunday," it's kind of the celebratory moment of levity in the midst of the dark days nearing solstice.

Of course, these days, all December is one long party, feast, shopping frenzy, you name it.

But what if you are a person who has lost someone in the past year? Or you're facing health issues, or recovering from addiction, or dealing with challenges in your relationships, or tuning in to the world's suffering and finding it so heavy and heartbreaking that you can scarcely breathe? Then the festivity rings pretty hollow—or worse, it creates a painfully grating sensation against all that we carry.

In that case, then you might need the third Sunday of Advent as a moment of relief against the short days and the dark nights. That's why we light a candle and commit to finding joy in the present, in the midst of the world as it is, not as we hope it is becoming.

Seeking joy in the midst of the world's chaos can be a spiritual discipline, an act of resistance.

As the poet Roethke said, "Deep in their roots, all flowers keep the light."

During the season of Advent, we light candles against the darkness, believing that darkness has a purpose and trusting that good things are taking shape in unseen places. We draw that light into the center of our being and store it up in our roots for the long winter ahead.

With the light of Christ at our core, we don't have to be afraid of the dark. We might even find joy there while we wait.

Merciful God, help us to trust that you are at work in unseen places, and teach us to be keepers of your light. May we find joy in every season to sustain us even in winter. Amen.

Week 3, Day 3

Sing praises to the LORD, O you his faithful ones,
    and give thanks to his holy name.
For his anger is but for a moment;
    his favor is for a lifetime.
Weeping may linger for the night,
    but joy comes with the morning.

— Psalm 30:4–5

This psalm hits different if you are a parent. If you've ever spent a long, miserable night awake and pacing the floor with a crying baby, you know that the weeping may literally last all night!

But then the sun comes up, and you see that sweet face (probably asleep now, of course). You see the perfect curve of the cheek, the tiny dimple, the soft spot that promises how much growth is possible. That sleeping baby might even have the nerve to open one eye and smile a sleepy smile at you, all drool and adorableness. And then, as exhausted as you are, you know joy. You make some coffee, and you try to live another day.

There are so many kinds of long nights awaiting all of us — even that baby, once she grows up. Long, dark nights of the soul, wrestling with addiction or mental illness; nights awaiting election results that may determine the fate of a nation or even the world; nights at the bedside of a loved one who is ill or dying; nights of doubt, physical pain, impossible work, or just lingering sleeplessness. This is the cost of living in fragile human form and of loving other humans just as fragile as we are.

But after each long night, the sun comes up. And maybe it comes through the window at just such an angle that we see some dust on the sunbeam and know that God loves fragile things too. Maybe it catches the corner of a water glass and casts a rainbow on the wall, and you remember that God has made all sorts of promises to her beloved creation.

As long as we live, there will be long nights. There will be weeping. There will be moments of fear and doubt. But joy comes in the morning. Joy comes as a baby who looks on us with such great love. Joy comes in the resilience of the human spirit that the holy one breathed into each of our lungs before we were born, thanks be to God.

Joyful Spirit, dwell with us all the days of our lives. Bring a glimpse of your goodness to our long nights and the promise of your faithfulness to our days of struggle. Amen.

Week 3, Day 4

Rejoice in the Lord always; again I will say, Rejoice. Let your gentleness be known to everyone. The Lord is near. Do not be anxious about anything, but in everything by prayer and supplication with thanksgiving let your requests be made known to God. . . . I can do all things through him who strengthens me.
— Philippians 4:4–6, 13

Paul's epistles to congregations in the early church are filled with words of encouragement. He is optimistic about the future, despite issues facing each local congregation, illness, political danger, and even his own imprisonment. Facing an uncertain fate, Paul had every reason to be afraid, and so did the outpost communities that were following his teachings. But still he tells them: rejoice!

There is something about "rejoice in the Lord always" that, in the wrong setting, sounds a lot like a passive-aggressive "you should smile more." There is such a thing as toxic positivity, and sometimes, passages like this pulled out of context can wander into that territory. Telling someone that they should rejoice, just choose to be happy, in spite of all circumstances, is at best tone-deaf and at worst cruel. We can't always just put a happy face on suffering, and the church that implies otherwise has wandered away from the gospel of Christ that is good news for the oppressed.

And yet . . .

Joy that is purely tied to our circumstances will always be fleeting. The joy found in deepest faith, on the other hand, can survive seasons of doubt and fear and can even help us rise above them.

Rejoice in the Lord always! It is an invitation and a reminder that there is always joy to be found in the promises of God, even if not in our immediate surroundings. The joyful moments that we find throughout the Advent season bear witness to the joy that is always ours to share. With that light at our disposal, we can "do all things" with the joy of Christ. And we have nothing to fear.

We give you thanks, Lord, for the joy that sustains us through trials and the joy that gives meaning to our days. From the smallest glimmers to the brightest fireworks, we seek you in every day, in every moment. Give us joy in this time of waiting as we receive your gift to the world. Amen.

Week 3, Day 5

Ring the bells that still can ring
....
There is a crack, a crack in everything.
That's how the light gets in.
— Leonard Cohen[5]

If we're being real, we know that much of the joy that happens at this time of year is purely manufactured. Stores are selling joy because the happier we feel, the more money we'll spend (often money we don't even have). There's a certain hypnosis in all the sparkling lights and tinsel. The voice of Mariah Carey or Bing Crosby on the speakers (in a constant loop, it seems) lulls us into a festive complacency where we can happily hand over our credit card and forget about the bill that's coming in mid-January. (Grab a Starbucks peppermint mocha to enjoy on your shopping trip, and the effects are manifold.)

That is in no way to say that you shouldn't enjoy those seasonal vibes to the fullest. Up against the cold weather, the shorter days, and the general heaviness of the world, sometimes a festive coffee drink and some Very Merry Mariah Carey are just what the doctor ordered! Fun family outings to look at lights or go ice skating are core memory material. All of this is important.

But our joy is not dependent on anything so circumstantial. The peace of this season need not rely on the peace of our surroundings. Our hope is not just in the things we experience with our senses. There might be years when we are ill and can't make these treks to our usual winter wonderlands. There are those who have no family to enjoy the season with them, and, Lord knows, there are those whose economic situation removes any of these experiences from reach.

The things that we enjoy this time of year may point us to the light, but they are certainly not the source of our joy. God's love incarnate is free and available to all. Or, put another way — if it's not free and available to all, then it isn't the true light of Christmas.

Enjoy the shiny lights and the favorite holiday experiences and the gifts, as you are able. But remember the true light of Christ that reaches us even in poverty, even in imperfection, even — maybe especially — in the depths of night and the places we find most fearful.

Jesus is born not to a world that is perfect but to our broken pieces and places. Through the cracks and fractures, the light breaks in — and it is good news for all.

Immanuel, God with us, we seek the joy of your perfect love. We give you thanks for every moment and opportunity that we have to celebrate and enjoy the gifts of this season, time with family and friends, the beauty of lights, and the anticipation of gifts. Let each of these glimpses point us to the greatest joy, which is your word made flesh: God with us. Amen.

FOURTH WEEK
OF ADVENT

Sacred Disruptions

We know it's coming, right? Every year, like clockwork, someone in your household is going to get sick over the holidays. Or there will be some inclement weather, and the power will go out just as you're ready to cook the turkey. Or the snow will mean you can't travel or someone can't travel to you. Or you do travel and the airline loses your bag, along with the perfect gift you brought and the ugly Christmas sweater that you wait all year to wear.

You name it—whatever variation on the theme, something is coming that will disrupt any lingering Norman Rockwell visions we might have in our heads about Christmas.

And what if your disruption is an unexpected guest like cousin Eddie in *National Lampoon's Christmas Vacation*? Not only does he show up unannounced, but he brings his whole family, his dog, his house on wheels, even his own septic system, which has to be emptied into the gutter in front of your house, for all the neighbors to see!

And it's not just the sewer scene. His signature bathrobe does not scream "family holiday photo" by any stretch. And there is something so unrefined about his manner that even if you were watching the movie for the first time, you would know that everything about this man is about to throw Clark's "perfect holiday plan" into comic chaos.

We love cousin Eddie though, do we not? The movie is nothing without him. We love his ear flaps, his ill-timed arrival, and his uncouth manner because in the movie—and in life in general—maybe the disruption is the point?

On a long ago night, near Bethlehem, there were shepherds, abiding in the field . . . and boy did their ordinary evening get disrupted!

The Shepherds' Angels

In those days a decree went out from Caesar Augustus that all the world should be registered. This was the first registration and was taken while Quirinius was governor of Syria. All went to their own towns to be registered. Joseph also went from the town of Nazareth in Galilee to Judea, to the city of David called Bethlehem, because he was descended from the house and family of David. He went to be registered with Mary, to whom he was engaged and who was expecting a child. While they were there, the time came for her to deliver her child. And she gave birth to her firstborn son and wrapped him in bands of cloth and laid him in a manger, because there was no place in the guest room.

Now in that same region there were shepherds living in the fields, keeping watch over their flock by night. Then an angel of the Lord stood before them, and the glory of the Lord shone around them, and they were terrified. But the angel said to them, "Do not be afraid, for see, I am bringing you good news of great joy for all the people: to you is born this day in the city of David a Savior, who is the Messiah, the Lord. This will be a sign for you: you will find a child wrapped in bands of cloth and lying in a manger." And suddenly there was with the angel a multitude of the heavenly host, praising God and saying,

> "Glory to God in the highest heaven,
>> and on earth peace among those whom he favors!"

When the angels had left them and gone into heaven, the shepherds said to one another, "Let us go now to Bethlehem and see this thing that has taken place, which the Lord has made known to us." So they went with haste and found Mary and Joseph and the child lying in the manger. When they saw this, they made known what had been told them about this child, and all who heard it were amazed at what the shepherds told them, and Mary treasured all these words and pondered them in her heart. The shepherds returned, glorifying and praising God for all they had heard and seen, just as it had been told them.

Luke 2:1–20

Talk about a disruption! These guys are minding their business, doing their everyday job, and then all of a sudden: surprise! The sky was alive with heavenly beings. They looked up from their flock to witness a sky full of dancing light, not with the usual constellations, but with a host of singing angels.

Scripture doesn't provide a lot of backstory on the shepherds here, but I'd venture a guess that "surprise" is the last thing they desired on a work night. I'd reckon that any number of surprises they encountered from time to time brought anything but good news. Wolves and other predators, thieves and others with ill-intent, storms and other acts of nature—those are just a few of the unwelcome surprises that they had to worry about on the clock. A sky full of angels? Not on their list of concerns. But certainly not on their wish list either!

This surprise is not a threat like a coyote or a sheep snatcher. This is a good and holy disruption. But still. How are the shepherds to know that? Given their professional experience with surprises, one can understand why their first reaction is to be terrified. On the surface, this is the thing that perhaps humans fear most of all: a stranger, the "other." But the angel said to them—surely we know this by now—"Do not be afraid!" The angels bring instead "good news of great joy!" A savior that looks a lot like a baby. And it just so happens that this particular baby is God's love made flesh, born to the weary world.

The nativity story is the story of the ultimate sacred disruption, of people who were neither true saints or blatant sinners (that we know of) but just as regular as could be. And as they were going about their business as usual, a miracle literally dropped from the sky. They had not been prepped for this moment in any way. They had no frame of reference for understanding what this meant for their lives or the world. But somehow, they were ready.

Once the angels dispersed, the shepherds talked among themselves and pretty quickly decided that they would go and see this thing the angels were singing about. They left their flock and hurried down to Bethlehem.

The rest, we might say, is history. They saw the child, and they went off to share the news with one and all. The news of a surprise visitor was now theirs to distribute.

I wonder how that happens—ordinary people figuring out how to let the holy disruption of "God with us" be a welcome guest, a surprise guest, instead of an intruder? The ability to make that distinction must be a powerful work of the Spirit. Because human impulse so often errs on the side of "stranger danger" when we encounter someone who is different from us, it takes some intention to cultivate a different kind of response to the unknown.

It takes some spiritual discipline, and a practice of opening ourselves up to the "other" in ways that run counter to our fight or flight instinct—and to our cultural conditioning as well.

It can be way too easy to sequester ourselves in homogenous pods these days. We do much of our communicating on the phone anyway. We may have a garage door opener in our car so that we can come and go from our homes without ever making eye contact with a neighbor. We can get our coffee, our lunch, our dry cleaning, and our banking services via drive-up window. Our communities are rarely walkable in ways that put us in the presence of one another. The appeal of (and options for) remote work continue to expand. For a fee, we can even make groceries magically appear on our doorstep! In other words, the more privilege and resources available to us, the more we can get through our day with minimal human encounters. So for all the ways we have evolved to better understand our beautiful, multicultural world, we have also devised ways to avoid encountering that world at all. We can go any number of days without talking to a stranger, or anyone at all.

But how much we miss.

A Welcome Stranger

A young man walked into the church basement. I assumed he was there for the class that I lead midweek with the men from the addiction recovery program in the neighborhood. Each Wednesday, we meet to work on spiritual practices that support the journey of the twelve-step program. I get to know the regulars pretty well, especially if they make it through the whole first phase of the residential program, and if they also come to worship on Sunday mornings. However, the program is something of a revolving door, so it would not have been surprising for someone to walk in that I didn't know.

But this young man walked in late and took a seat on the bench near the wall. I realized that none of the other men knew him either, and things got awkward quickly. It turns out he was looking for assistance with food, but here he had walked into a whole group of strangers.

I didn't want to keep him waiting for another forty-five minutes, which was how much class time we had left, but I couldn't walk away from the class I was leading in order to assist the unexpected guest. So we invited him to join us.

While the guest was unexpected, I tried not to make him feel unwelcome. I quickly explained what the class was and who we all were, and then I tried as best I could to move on with the discussion. But the flow had been disrupted, and it felt difficult to transition back to what we'd been doing.

Within about ten minutes of sitting in with us, however, the young man shared that his mother struggles with a heroin addiction and that he had recently moved home from college in order to take care of his two younger sisters. It was a truly devastating story of suffering, grief, sacrifice, and uncertainty. In so many ways, this young man was experiencing all the things we humans fear the most. And here he was, sharing it with a roomful of strangers with the deepest vulnerability.

His situation hit close to home for the other men in the room. They might have met him with judgment, avoidance, or some other fearful response. But instead, they gave him so much support and encouragement. They gave him hope. They affirmed how he was caring for his family. They offered unconditional love to a stranger who had wandered into their midst.

We sent our guest home later with a grocery card and an open invitation to return. It was such an ordinary day, all things considered. But we'd also witnessed the mystery and miracle of someone having wandered into exactly the right place at the right time. When the house was full, the door was unlocked, and the Spirit was moving in all the right ways for a stranger to find welcome with fellow travelers who met him unafraid.

We know that the unexpected bumps, the unforeseen plan changes, and the strangers at the door are going to happen, whether we are ready or not. Life goes a lot better for us, and the world is a better place, if we can become "yay, surprise guest!" people instead of "oh no, uninvited visitor" kind of folks.

If we want to really cultivate that kind of mindset, we'd do well to remember not only that some angels showed up as a holy disruption in the night sky for some shepherds once but also that Jesus, himself, was a stranger. He was born to parents who were on the road with no place to stay. No room for them in the inn.

Scholars now say that it wasn't exactly a Holiday Inn type of place where Mary and Joseph were turned away because there was no room, but likely a family home where lots of folks were staying, coming and going at all hours due to the activity in the town nearby. The Greek word *kataluma* has traditionally been translated as "inn." But, as biblical scholar Eric Smith says, "a *kataluma* is now understood less as a hotel room or a room in an inn, and more as a spare room or guest room in someone's house. . . . Most likely, Mary and Joseph had landed at the crowded house of some relatives. Instead of having a private space (which would have been in short supply in most houses of that day), they are in the big common space of their relatives' house. . . . Likely it was a hybrid space, where people, stuff, and livestock mixed."[1]

With this in mind, the birthplace of Jesus sounds less like the barn behind a chain motel and more like a place where everyday life was happening and all sorts of people were making "get in where you fit in" lodgings work as best they could. Extended family, friends, and guests were just going about their ordinary business when a baby was born into their midst. One more unplanned-for visitor to join the chaos. Welcome to the world, kid.

Love shows up for us, just like this, all the time. The stranger at the door. The baby born in its own good time. The event or trip that goes off schedule in all the right ways. The uninvited cousin whose ear flaps and bathrobe aren't photo-ready but who's about to bring the real spirit of Christmas to what would otherwise be a stuffy and joyless family feast.

Love shows up as a young man who needs support and some grocery money. It comes to town undocumented. It appears as an unhoused neighbor in worship, a refugee family new to the neighborhood, or a baby born to the family that's just passing through.

The question is always, ever, only this: Will we be ready?

Will we welcome love, however it comes to us, unafraid?

Discuss and Reflect

*Find a Spotify playlist and chapter introduc-
tion videos to use during group study or private
meditation at:*

www.wjkbooks.com/CallingAllAngels

— Has an unexpected guest ever disrupted your
  "business as usual" holiday plans?
— How can we cultivate our readiness for surprises
  and prepare to be amazed by them rather than
  afraid?
— Why do you think God sent the angels to
  shepherds and not to a rabbi or other faith
  leader? Would a religious official have
  responded differently?
— Can you think of some other examples of "holy
  disruptions" in the life of the church or in the
  community where you live?
— How might love disrupt our everyday reality
  right now? And how can choosing love help us
  overcome the fearful parts of living in these times?

Activity Idea for This Week

With your family, church group, or any combi-
nation of friends and neighbors, plan a day of
service together. Note that many organizations
doing important work in your community are
overwhelmed with volunteers at this time of year,
but they need help all year long. If serving this
particular week doesn't work with their schedule

(or yours), find a day in January and go ahead and get it on everyone's calendars. You probably already have a cause or organization that is near and dear to your heart. If not, now is a great time to do some research and see who is doing good work in your community, particularly in regard to welcoming strangers and making a place for those who have no place (think refugee ministries or services for people experiencing homelessness). Learn not only what kind of work they are doing but also how you can best support their impact. Whatever avenue you choose, you are finding ways to tangibly share the light and love of Christ — not just in the Advent and Christmas season but in ordinary time as well.

DAILY REFLECTIONS

Week 4, Day 1

For he will command his angels concerning you
  to guard you in all your ways.
On their hands they will bear you up,
  so that you will not dash your foot against a stone.
You will tread on the lion and the adder;
  the young lion and the serpent you will trample
    under foot.

Those who love me, I will deliver;
  I will protect those who know my name.
When they call to me, I will answer them;
  I will be with them in trouble;
  I will rescue them and honor them.
With long life I will satisfy them
  and show them my salvation.
                                        —Psalm 91:11–16

The fact that so many of the psalms mention fear reminds us just how pervasive a force fear has always been in human experience. Fear is not a sign of unfaithfulness or weakness, and it is certainly not a sin.

What can become sinful is how we respond to fear.

Fear is one of the five main characters in the original *Inside Out*—that brilliant Disney/Pixar movie that features the five driving emotions inside a young girl's mind as she goes through the emotional upheaval of a cross-country move. *Fear* is the purple guy. Voiced by Bill Hader, he is often cowering in the corner and telling all the other feelings to *stop* and *stay here* and *don't touch anything*. Which is to say, if we let fear do the driving all the time, we will literally never go anywhere.

Fortunately, in the movie—and hopefully, in our own lives—other emotions help buffer the instinct of fear. Joy, especially, often took over and made sure that the young girl got out and lived her life and even had fun!

All of our own worst impulses are driven by fear. Fear of not having enough leads to greed. Fear of being judged leads us to judge others first. Fear of death leads us to defy it by doing stupid, risky things just to prove our bodies are invincible. (Spoiler alert: they're not.) Fear of outsiders coming to take what's "ours"? Build a wall! Send them home!

Fear may be a powerful force in the world. But as the psalmists so often remind us, love is even more powerful than fear.

We cannot control how the forces of evil use fear to manipulate, and we cannot entirely control how our communities and world are shaped by fear. But what we can control is our own response to fear. What we can remember is that God has promised to deliver those who love him, to answer those who call for help.

We can remember that responding to fear with greater love is perhaps the most transformative act imaginable.

God of love, hear our prayer: that the world might be shaped by a love that casts out fear; that our own hearts might be transformed by the abiding love of a savior. Amen.

Week 4, Day 2

Beloved, let us love one another, because love is from God; everyone who loves is born of God and knows God. Whoever does not love does not know God, for God is love. God's love was revealed among us in this way: God sent his only Son into the world so that we might live through him. . . .

There is no fear in love, but perfect love casts out fear; for fear has to do with punishment, and whoever fears has not reached perfection in love. We love because he first loved us. Those who say, "I love God," and hate a brother or sister are liars, for those who do not love a brother or sister, whom they have seen, cannot love God, whom they have not seen. The commandment we have from him is this: those who love God must love their brothers and sisters also.

—1 John 4:7–9, 18–21

"There is no fear in love." Say that again for the folks in the back!

"Perfect love casts out fear." Let's hear that one again too!

The great tragedy of Christianity is how much fear has played a part in the marketing.

People are leaving church in droves, and we can lament all day long that people can't find time for God anymore, that folks don't have their priorities right, that the schedules of the retail world and youth sports leagues have destroyed faith in America. But anecdotally, I can say most people who leave the church go because what they do believe about God is utterly at odds with the toxic theology they were raised with in church.

I can also attest that much of my ministry is spent "unteaching" the harmful things that people learned as children. *As children.*

LGBTQ people have heard from churches that there was something sinful and flawed in their very being and that God would punish them by letting them suffer eternally. I've met people in recovery who say that childhood images of hell and the devil scarred them for life — and often even *played a role in their turning to substances for escape.* People who lost a parent or sibling who "wasn't saved" may spend years trying to shake the dread of their loved one sentenced to the fiery pit for all eternity.

This list could go on and on. The point is, there is real trauma in how some faith leaders have packaged the Christian narrative over time (and up to today). *But these harmful messages are rooted entirely in fear.* Fear can be used as a means of control, to manipulate church attendance and, Lord forgive us, to keep the funds flowing through the offering plate. Who would want to be a part of a faith like that, much less devote their life to it?

If perfect love casts out fear — and Jesus Christ is, above all, the embodiment of perfect love — then fear has no place in our teachings of him and certainly no place in the communities committed to following him.

What if the body of Christ was as attached to loving the world as it has historically been to shame, fear, and control? What if we made it our life's mission to banish all threat of punishment and instead bear witness to the love of Christ through acts of service, unthinkable generosity, and radical hospitality?

We love because he first loved us. So very much.

Merciful God, forgive us for the ways your church has fallen short of embodying your love and amazing hope. We ask healing for all those who have sought acceptance and mercy and who have found only fear and judgment instead. May they find new faith in the perfect love that is born to the world at Christmas. Send your Spirit to cast out all fear among us so that all may walk in the ways of love. Amen.

Week 4, Day 3

But now thus says the LORD,
   he who created you, O Jacob,
   he who formed you, O Israel:
Do not fear, for I have redeemed you;
   I have called you by name; you are mine.
When you pass through the waters, I will be with
      you,
   and through the rivers, they shall not overwhelm
      you;
when you walk through fire you shall not be burned,
   and the flame shall not consume you.

. . . .

Do not remember the former things
   or consider the things of old.
I am about to do a new thing;
   now it springs forth; do you not perceive it?
I will make a way in the wilderness
   and rivers in the desert.

                              —Isaiah 43:1–2, 18–19

The first few Decembers I spent in Arizona were weird.

Having spent my whole life in my home state of Kentucky, I moved to Phoenix for my first solo pastor gig when I was in my late twenties. Aside from the brutally hot summers, I loved everything about it. But there were many elements of culture and climate that took some big time getting used to.

Like, for instance, the fact that Christmastime did not precisely happen in winter. At least winter as I knew it!

December in Phoenix is actually quite perfect — lots of blue skies, an occasional nip in the air, and plenty of sunshine. After suffering through the long, hot summer months (and more hot months when it is supposed to be fall), "winter" is glorious!

But it's not exactly Bing Crosby territory. It really took some adjusting to lead a church through Advent and prep for Christmas services while wearing sandals and having all the windows open. (Now I am back in Kentucky, where December means twenty degrees with three inches of snow on the ground, and what I wouldn't give for some Phoenix "Christmas" weather right about now!)

I don't know that I ever got used to the different seasonal rhythms out there. But what I did learn was a deep appreciation for the wilderness side of the Advent journey. Particularly the fact that right around the time I was used to everything dying and turning brown, the desert was just waking up from months of oppressive heat, and it was just full of green, growing things.

Any time it rained in the winter, succulents would get brighter and all kinds of things would bloom or pop up out of the ground, as if everything was so dang thirsty and just waiting for the smallest splash of water so that the earth could start breathing again.

I got in the habit of taking a long walk in the desert preserve by my house on the afternoon of Christmas Eve. I would marvel at how much life could thrive in such an inhospitable landscape and how, even in wilderness, things could be born.

The promises of the prophet Isaiah ring so true in this season, even though I'm back in a place where winter is on time and means business. God truly brings water to the driest of places, holy disruptions to old things, former things, all the things that we are used to that might be holding us back and preventing our growth.

God is doing new things for us, and within us, all the time. Change is so often the thing that we fear deeply, but the Spirit grants us endless capacity to bloom where we're planted and to learn new ways of experiencing ancient things. Can we trust that this is good news?

As the legend herself, Emmylou Harris, sings on my very favorite Christmas album: "It will rain, it will rain, in the desert."[2]

God, we give you thanks for the changing seasons and for providing for us even in wilderness places. Grant us faith that endures change and sustains us through times of uncertainty. May we trust that you are doing new things all the time and accept your invitation to take part in the new creation all around us. Amen.

Week 4, Day 4

Let love be genuine; hate what is evil; hold fast
to what is good; love one another with mutual
affection; outdo one another in showing honor.
Do not lag in zeal; be ardent in spirit; serve the
Lord. Rejoice in hope; be patient in affliction;
persevere in prayer. Contribute to the needs of
the saints; pursue hospitality to strangers.

— Romans 12:9–13

It was a very cold night. The family had traveled for
many days over treacherous terrain, and they were
so weary; but there was no room for them. Everyone else had been traveling too, and everyone was
cold, and everyone needed a place to rest. Beds and
warmth were commodities hard to come by.

The family joined a long line of others who had
recently come into town, not entirely sure of what
they were waiting on, or who would meet them, or
what help the strangers might be able to offer.

Finally, at the head of a long queue, some kind
folks showed the family through a door and into a
warm room where a bed had been prepared with
fresh linens, a place set for them at the table, a hot
meal served with care.

Because on that very cold Christmas Eve night,
when they could have been home by the fire or out
doing some last-minute shopping, church people
in El Paso, Texas, opened their doors to migrants
who had just crossed the border. They knew that
on a night so cold, shelter beds would be hard
to come by. Harder still for the undocumented,

because while the city had set up various emergency shelters, only those who turned themselves in to border patrol and had the paperwork to show for it were allowed to stay in the shelters. Many were, of course, afraid to do so.[3] But all around the border town (and others like it, all across the southwest), God's people chose to welcome the Christ of Christmas by welcoming migrants and giving them shelter, no questions asked.

Because God's people opened the door, a migrant family—young parents with a baby boy—did not have to brave the cold alone as strangers in a strange land.

It happens like this. Love comes and lives among us. It meets us right where we are.

God, let the love we profess be genuine, spoken in word and acted in deed. Give us the courage to act on our love and not just speak it. Amen.

Week 4, Day 5

Let mutual affection continue. Do not neglect to show hospitality to strangers, for by doing that some have entertained angels without knowing it.

—Hebrews 13:1–2

Yong Cha Prince was ready to close the Western Motor Inn in Denver, which she had run with her husband for many years. After the death of her husband, as well as their young adult son, she was ready to return home to South Korea.

But the night before the closure, a woman appeared at her door. She had six Venezuelan boys with her, and they had no place to go. Yong Cha invited them to stay for free.

But there were more.

Migrant children came to the motel, as well as adults who had arrived in the city that year and were finding it hard to stay warm since the weather had turned cold. Within just a few days, every room was full. There were nearly three hundred guests.[4]

The innkeeper, along with Christina Asuncion, who found and brought those first boys to the door, continued working to house and feed as many of their neighbors as they possibly could. Read the full story[5] as the gospel that it is—God's people continuing to bear witness to love made flesh, even in the most difficult circumstances.

Of course, the building had many problems—that's part of why Prince was ready to close it. And of course, feeding hundreds of people a day is more expense than two women alone can cover. That's why members of the community have chipped in to help. The ongoing challenges facing this extraordinary effort indicate that it's going to take a village to keep it going.

But that it even got off the ground is a miracle. This story could have gone so many different ways. Christina might have been afraid when she encountered those boys in the local park, and she could have walked the other way. Yong Cha might have been afraid to open her door to strangers. She might have been afraid to stay in a place that held so much sadness for her. The neighbors might have been afraid and protested the whole thing.

But one took the boys to the door. The other said yes, come in, we have room. They both stayed and kept opening that door again and again.

And instead of protesting, the neighbors came to help.

Just look what can happen when people live unafraid.

Here is the good news of love made flesh: love doesn't have to wait until we are perfectly ready and available, until we have all the plans in place and all the supplies ordered and the roof fixed. Love doesn't have to wait until we have enough money or enough hands or enough energy or perfect faith. Love comes to the door, to meet us as we are, asking only that we do the same.

God with us, Immanuel, the room is ready and the places are set. Come to us, abide with us, take your place in our hearts and our homes. May we always be ready and waiting when angels come calling, and may we never fail to welcome strangers with the love and welcome we have known in you. Amen.

CHRISTMAS

Escape to Egypt

On December 7, 1914—in the midst of what we now call World War I—Pope Benedict XV proposed an official Truce of God in which all hostilities would cease over the Christmas season. Military leaders rejected the idea.

Still, on Christmas Eve night, German soldiers on the battlefield lit candles; they even put up trees in the trenches! And they began singing carols. British soldiers, in trenches of their own, began singing back. In other places, battle raged on. But here, the men began to emerge and shake hands, exchange Christmas greetings, some even taking pictures together. History has named this shining moment in the midst of war the Christmas Eve Truce of 1914. Fiona Bevin wrote a song about it.[1] And I bet if you've been to more than one Christmas Eve service in your life, you've heard it used in a sermon somewhere. It's a beautiful story, reflecting the very best of human nature.

As is so often the case with a great story, historical accounts do not agree on the details around this night. Discrepancies persist around the precise location and how many soldiers were involved. Some even say there was some great soccer played that night. That may or may not be true, and it is hard to separate fact from legend in a tale that has been recounted so many times (much as with Scripture itself).

What we do know is that this was not the first truce of its kind, but it was possibly the last in a conflict that continued to rage for a long time after that brief silent night. However historical accounts may differ, that one night was not to be the end of the war. In fact, the war was just beginning.[2]

What a beautiful and terrible story. Beautiful for the obvious reasons: the Prince of Peace is born to the world and humans actually lay down their weapons and share in the joy and peace of the occasion together. It's also deeply tragic that, at some point after that lovely moment, the soldiers picked up their weapons and went right back to the violence, back to the path of least resistance and reliance on human mechanisms of power.

Such a temporary peace is a painful reminder that God's time is not the same as our time. We learn this, in some way, in every liturgical season. God's time is not our time—and in God's time, two things can be true at once. All of our hope and fear, our human faith and our doubt—it is all wrapped up in time and often coexists in the same space.

I was thinking of that short-lived WWI Christmas truce when, on Christmas morning of 2023, Israeli forces dropped bombs on Bethlehem. Just hours after U.S. churches lit candles and sang "Silent Night," violence shook the physical place of Jesus' birth and forced the cancellation of Christmas worship services and other celebrations in the surrounding communities. That day brought the death toll of Palestinians to a staggering twenty thousand. There was no truce of any kind on that Christmas day.

In the days leading up to that moment, with violence already raging, artist Kelly Latimore rendered an image: "Christ in the Rubble."[3] It depicts the holy family huddled under a pile of debris, with buildings on fire behind and around them. Following the Christmas bombings, the image made for an even more stunning picture of how the world greets the Prince of Peace.

The light of the holy family's halos seem to hold up the rubble around them. They are trapped, but they are not crushed entirely.

The Holy Family's Angel

Now after [the wise men] had left, an angel of the Lord appeared to Joseph in a dream and said, "Get up, take the child and his mother, and flee to Egypt, and remain there until I tell you, for Herod is about to search for the child, to destroy him." Then Joseph got up, took the child and his mother by night, and went to Egypt and remained there until the death of Herod. This was to fulfill what had been spoken by the Lord through the prophet, "Out of Egypt I have called my son."

—Matthew 2:13–15

Lest we forget—because the world will certainly try and make us forget—Jesus was a refugee in his early childhood.

I've often wondered if the angel that appeared to Joseph and told him to take his family and flee to Egypt was the same angel that showed up on a different night and told him to take Mary as his wife and raise the child she carried as his own flesh and blood. Matthew, though reluctant to name his angels, surely sees them acting in similar fashion and for a common purpose. These angels appear in dreams, and they bring a message not just of hypothetical courage and strength but of very practical instruction as well.

In this case, the instruction is simple: run.

The angel warns Joseph that King Herod is, in the fearful rage that only the powerful can feel when their power is threatened, intent on finding and killing the boy. Jesus, now about two years old, needs to get out of town, his family with him, and quick. Though the encounter is brief, the angel tells Joseph exactly where to go and why.

They go. And like so many families before them and since, they are now among the displaced.

The world wants us to forget this part of the story, because people in power gain leverage by putting up fences and building up walls. Whether they act out of their own fear or they play on the fear of their constituents (often both things are true), the result is the same: barriers that exist to keep out those most in need of refuge.

Between the years of 2016 and 2020, the U.S. refugee resettlement program, once among the strongest in the world, was all but decimated, reaching a record low of fifteen thousand entries in 2020.[4] (Some of those placements were not even utilized.) That ceiling has since been raised to the 125,000 range, more in line with the recent history of the modern refugee program.

By mid-2023, there were 110 million forcibly displaced people around the globe. That reflects a consistent and steady increase over the last two decades. It's very likely that, by the time this book is in your hands, that number will be higher. That's 110 million children of God around the world who are waiting in camps, living in temporary shelters and communities of necessity. Some have been displaced by conflict, others by poverty and climate change. Some live in temporary shelters with access to education, fresh water, and career opportunities, while others are beyond the reach of humanitarian aid and woefully lacking in resources. And some, like the young Jesus, are targets of political violence.

With the number of displaced people around the world now at an all-time high (and climbing), this text from Matthew's Gospel is a painful reminder that the trauma Jesus and his family endured thousands of years ago remains all too common in human experience. By all logic, that parallel should sound the alarm for Christians to respond to this crisis with great urgency and radical compassion. The safety and dignity of refugees should transcend any political allegiances for people of faith. And yet . . . party lines have been drawn, and people of faith too often seem to find themselves on opposite sides of it in regard to this critical matter.

Many are afraid: either afraid to let unknown immigrants from far-off places through our borders and into our communities or afraid to stand up to world leaders who still grasp for power at the expense of humans in need. Some may even be afraid that if congregations get too active in the work of welcoming refugees, they'll be accused of being political, and thus fear losing members.

The cognitive dissonance is frankly stunning—that some churches can sing "Away in a Manger" about the little Lord Jesus and his sweet head and in the same breath celebrate the brand of American nationalism and exceptionalism that actively opposes resettlement.

At the same time, many Western communities of faith have rallied to take part in resettling families through their local partner agencies. There is great hope to be found in those congregations (and mosques, and temples) that are not bound by fear; in these places, God's people live as if they have heard and believe the story of love made flesh, and they know God came into the world in the most vulnerable form imaginable: a refugee child.

What any faith community involved in refugee resettlement will tell you is this: they serve in this way not just because their faith calls them to welcome the stranger but also because their faithful response enriches their own community of faith. Working closely with resettled neighbors and helping them find their way for the next part of the journey opens groups that are otherwise homogenous to expansive possibilities for ministry.

The manufacturing town of Utica, New York, once

had a population of around one hundred thousand. That number began to plunge in the 1960s, and over the next several decades, homes were abandoned or destroyed. Then refugees from Bosnia, who had education and building skills, began moving to town, buying those homes for a low price and fixing them up. Then in the early 2000s, a new surge of refugees from Myanmar (formerly known as Burma) also began to settle in the community. Resettled refugees now make up about a quarter of Utica's population and a sizable part of the local workforce.[5]

Just as the declining Rust-Belt town of Utica, New York, has been transformed by the presence of refugees in the community, congregations find a new vitality most any time they open themselves up to the cultures, experiences, and stories of those who are seeking new life. It's not a matter of converting refugees to Christianity and adding to the overall worship attendance. It's more that openness to the other, rather than fearfulness of them, always yields some sort of new life.

The great surprise is what that new life will be.

Christ in the Rubble

In the midst of the rubble of Bethlehem in 2023, Rev. Dr. Munther Isaac delivered a Christmas sermon at the Evangelical Lutheran Christmas Church in Bethlehem. His message, also titled "Christ in the Rubble," pointed to the resilience of a baby born into a place of suffering: "Resilience because this very same child, rose up from the midst of pain, destruction, darkness and death to challenge Empires, to speak truth to power and deliver an everlasting victory over death and darkness."[6]

In that same sermon, Dr. Isaac called out Western leaders and, particularly, Western people of faith for their role in the ongoing violence. "Let it be clear: Silence is complicity, and empty calls for peace without a ceasefire and end to occupation, and the shallow words of empathy without direct action—are all under the banner of complicity."[7]

This is a powerful Christmas message about the power of incarnation, "God with us," born for the most desperate needs of humanity. It is also a prophetic word that is difficult to hear for people who live in comfort and can easily turn off the news rather than learn the depths and complexity of the global situation.

In God's time, two seemingly opposed truths can exist at once. Perhaps even many truths.

The world is at war, and yet the peace of Christ is ours at all times.

There is suffering and heartbreak and violence everywhere we look, and yet the love of God enfolds all living things.

Darkness casts shadows of poverty, hatred, fear, and greed. And yet a light shines in the darkness, and the darkness does not overcome it. Ever.

Soldiers can lay down their weapons for a night, only to pick them up again the next morning. Even so, there's something miraculous about a brief flash of light on that dim horizon. Light that was, for a moment, not gunfire or an exploding bomb but the light of Christmas candles, the light of peace, maybe the very light of God.

This is the great gift of God's time, that paradox

where two things can be true at once: God's peace is not yet realized, and yet it exists in the midst of all that is, and whatever else might be. This is the not-yet and already-becoming kingdom of heaven in our midst.

Given his childhood trauma as part of a displaced family fleeing political violence, Jesus might have spent the rest of his life living in fear. With such a beginning, having to flee from those who wanted to hurt him, he could have asked the angels to set him a sanctuary someplace where he could live his life in seclusion. But, in fact, his life would embody the very antithesis of fear. He would walk instead in the ways of prayer, justice, compassion, peace, community, and transforming love.

And with his whole life, he showed us how to go and do the same. How amazing is that?

The light of Christ cannot be overcome by human fear or fear's terrible consequences, because that light has already conquered even death. It's a light that lives within each of us so that we can face the forces of death with defiant hope and courage. And if death has no hold on us, then surely we need not be afraid of the dark.

Where will you go, and what will you do now that you are unafraid?

WORSHIP RESOURCES

In this section, pastors and worship leaders will find liturgies and other resources for each Sunday of Advent and Christmas Eve. Feel free to use or adapt these as needed for your context. Visit www.wjkbooks.com/callingallangels for slides to project or use in online worship.

For the Sundays of Advent, these resources include a Call to Worship, Communion Prayer, and, between them, a script for a joint Advent Candle Lighting and Children's Time. In many worship settings, a different family lights the Advent candle and does the reading each Sunday of the season. This is a lovely tradition, but it might also create one more moment for non-traditional families and single people to feel left out of the life of the church. In the interest of removing those barriers, I've opted in recent years to do the lighting of the Advent wreath as the children's sermon each week. This allows all of the children to participate, even if their family is not in the lineup to lead worship this year, and any who may be wary of church because of its focus on the traditional family model will not feel excluded. If you want to skip the children's sermon portion of this liturgy, go straight to the Advent candle lighting, which can be read by people of all ages.

For Christmas Eve, you will find a Call to Worship, a "Welcoming Light into the World" liturgy (during which the four candles of the Advent wreath are lit, as well as the Christ candle), a Christmas Prayer for a Weary World, and a Communion Prayer.

FIRST SUNDAY OF ADVENT

Call to Worship

One: Let us keep watch! Hear what the Lord
will say to us in these days.

**All: We need a good word for right now,
but we can't hear God's voice
over our own noise.**

One: The proud and the wealthy
don't have the right spirit;
the arrogant will never understand.

**All: So let us be humble and generous,
listening before we speak
and giving more than we receive.**

One: The Lord is in his holy temple.
Let all mortal flesh keep silence
before God.

**All: We will keep silent and not be afraid.
We will be still and wait for a word.**

One: Rejoice, O daughter Zion.
The Lord will come dwell in your midst,
and none will be afraid.

**All: Let all living things be silent
before the Lord.**[1]

Candle-Lighting Liturgy and Children's Time

Have you ever had to be quiet when you really, really, really felt like talking, shouting, and running around? (*Let kids discuss for a moment.*)

Well, we all have a hard time being quiet some-times, even grown-ups.

Advent is a time of waiting and preparation. Sometimes, our preparations are noisy. We have parties, we sing lots of songs, we might wrap presents and crinkle lots of paper. We might bake cookies and bang pots and pans around the kitchen!

But sometimes, it is time to be quiet and remember that what we're waiting for is . . . (*pause to ask children what we are waiting for*) for Jesus to be born (among other things children might share). So it's important that we don't get so busy and so loud that we forget all about the baby who's coming!

In the Bible, there are angels that appear to people who are waiting for Jesus to be born. And they always say, "Do not be afraid." Today we're going to light the candle of hope, and be quiet for a little bit, and think about how Jesus' coming means we don't have anything to be afraid of.

But before we're quiet, we're going to get loud—just to get it out of our system! (*Share festive noisemakers with the children.*) On the count of three, we're going to make noise as if it's a party, because we're so excited Jesus is coming—then we're going to put these away until Christmas, when we can get them back out again. (*Count down and then share in the noisemaking party.*)

And . . . stop.

OK, we will put these away. (*Collect noisemakers, using a special Christmas box or gift bag if available.*) And when it's time for Jesus to be born, we can celebrate some more. But now we are going to quietly walk over to the Advent wreath.

Notice the difference in the noise and the quiet? Do you notice that the quiet is peaceful? That we can slow down our breathing and be calm? Now we are ready to hear a word from God.

Reader 1: The LORD is my light and my
salvation;
whom shall I fear?
The LORD is the stronghold of my life;
of whom shall I be afraid?
. . . .
One thing I asked of the LORD;
this I seek:
to live in the house of the LORD
all the days of my life,
to behold the beauty of the LORD,
and to inquire in his temple.

For he will hide me in his shelter
in the day of trouble;
he will conceal me under the cover
of his tent;
he will set me high on a rock.
. . . .
I believe that I shall see the goodness
of the LORD
in the land of the living.
Wait for the LORD;
be strong, and let your heart take
courage;
wait for the LORD![2]

Reader 2: Today we light a candle to remind us
that hope is stronger than fear. As
we wait for the birth of the Christ
child, we will remember to find quiet

moments along the way so that we
can listen for God's word.

Reader 3: Let us pray: God, our hope is in you.
Help us to listen for your word so
that we will be ready to share the
good news of Jesus with others.
Thank you for the gifts of this season, for all the ways we can worship
you and serve others while we wait.
Amen.

Communion Prayer

God of the abundant table, forgive us when
we pretend there is not enough room here:
when we haggle over the guest list and
the seating arrangements though you have
called us only to set the table. As we wait
for Christ to be born among us again, teach
us to make more room, not less. May we
learn to see Jesus in the least and the last,
and may we bring that seat to the head of
the table. Bless this bread for our bodies,
that we might be restored for the work of
your kingdom; bless this cup for our spirits,
that we might be renewed for the work of
your word. Amen.

SECOND SUNDAY OF ADVENT

Call to Worship

One: Magnify the Lord, for she has done great things. She is mindful of the least and the last.

All: We praise the one who builds up the poor and casts down the powerful.

One: A child is coming who will turn the world upside down. Let us be like his mother and worship while we wait.

All: We worship God, who performs mighty deeds with her arm and gives voice to the outcast.

One: She fills the hungry with good things and sends the rich away empty.

All: We will wait and not be afraid.

Candle-Lighting Liturgy and Children's Time

Do you have a favorite Christmas song? (*Ask, "What are some of your favorite Christmas songs? And then let children discuss.*)

There are many different kinds of Christmas songs, but there are some words and ideas that come up over and over again! Can you think of any words that we hear a lot in our Christmas songs? (*Some words to share along with the children are "jolly," "sleigh," "snow," "merry," "angel," and "bright." If it works in your context, you might want to let the kids sing a song such as "Frosty the Snowman" or "Away in a Manger."*)

Many of the songs we sing at this time of year are about celebrating and having a good time. That's important!

Most of the songs we sing in church at this time of year have to do with what Jesus' birth means for us. When she was pregnant with Jesus, Mary even sang a song about what amazing things God was doing and would continue to do through Jesus. Some of our songs are also about light—like the light of our candles in worship and the Light of the World that is coming to us. And lots of our Christmas songs are also about peace, because Jesus is called the Prince of Peace. Today we light the candle of peace. We light the way for Jesus, and we keep the light of peace until he comes.

Reader 1: The people who walked in darkness
  have seen a great light;
those who lived in a land of deep
  darkness—
  on them light has shined.
You have multiplied exultation;
  you have increased its joy;
they rejoice before you
  as with joy at the harvest,
  as people exult when dividing
   plunder.
For the yoke of their burden
  and the bar across their shoulders,
  the rod of their oppressor,
  you have broken as on the day of
   Midian.

. . . .

For a child has been born for us,
a son given to us;
authority rests upon his shoulders,
and he is named
Wonderful Counselor, Mighty God,
Everlasting Father, Prince of Peace.[3]

Reader 2: As we light this candle of peace,
we remember that peace for the
world begins with peace in our
own hearts. We wait for the Prince
of Peace, who will show us the
way to end all war. Let peace
begin with me—let peace begin
with each one of us.

Reader 3: Let us pray: God, in you we find
true and everlasting peace. While
we wait for peace to reign on
earth, teach us to hold the light of
peace in our own hearts, to love
our neighbors, and to follow in the
way of Jesus, the Prince of Peace.
Amen.

Communion Prayer

God of mercy, we give you thanks for the
peace of this table where all may gather,
where the hungry are filled with good things,
and where we wait in hope together. Until
that day when your peace is made known on
the earth, fill us with the certainty of your love
made known in broken bread

and poured-out cup. Bless these elements to renew us in body and spirit as we follow in the way of Christ, the Prince of Peace. Amen.

THIRD SUNDAY OF ADVENT

Call to Worship

One: Now the Lord who made you
has this to say: "Do not fear,
for I have redeemed you.
I have called you by name
and you are mine."

**All: We hear the one who calls us by name,
but we are still so often afraid.**

One: May the spirit of God move in this place:
the spirit of faith, not fear; the spirit
of looking ahead and not backward.

**All: Lord, remind us again that you walk
with us, whether we pass through
the waters or walk through fire.**

One: We will not fix our eyes on the former
things but point our gaze toward the
new miracles that God is working for us!

All: We will look ahead and be unafraid.[4]

Candle-Lighting Liturgy and Children's Time

We're going to try something different today: we're
going to walk up to the Advent wreath like usual, but
we're going to walk backward. (*Help kids walk backward
up the aisle and/or chancel steps to where the advent wreath is.
If you have a child who is disabled or there are other challenges, modify as needed for your space.*) It can be tricky to
navigate walking backward, so I'm going to give you
something to help. (*Give the children each a small mirror,*

or give one large mirror to an older child to hold for the whole group.) This way, you can look in the mirror to watch behind you and see where you are going.

(*Wait for everyone to reach the chancel/Advent wreath before resuming the sermon.*) Was it a little harder than usual to get here? (*Discuss with the youth what was challenging.*)

There are several times in the Bible when the prophets remind people that it's not good to be looking backward all the time. People had a bad habit of being so focused on the past that they couldn't understand God was always doing things right now. It was like walking backward or looking over their shoulder with a mirror: it kept them from doing anything new or planning for the future. As we know, it's much easier to move forward when you are looking ahead, not back behind you!

During Advent, we are getting ready for one of God's new miracles: Jesus is born, not for the past, but for the present and the future. We light the candle of joy today, because it is a joy to be right here where we are and not always looking behind us.

Reader 1: But as for you, have no fear, my servant Jacob, says the LORD, and do not be dismayed, O Israel; for I am going to save you from far away and your offspring from the land of their captivity. Jacob shall return and have quiet and ease, and no one shall make him afraid. For I am with you, says the LORD, to save you.[5]

Reader 2: Today we light the candle of joy. We celebrate in big ways and small ways as we wait for Jesus, the Light of the World, to come to us. The greatest joy is being with the people we love and being grateful for all that we have, right this minute.

Reader 3: Let us pray: God, we sometimes have a hard time looking ahead. We worry about what we have forgotten, or what we have done wrong, or what we have not done at all. Help us to let go of the past and look forward, trusting in the new things you are doing all the time. We give you thanks for the joy of this season and for all the ways we can bring joy to others while we wait. Amen.

Communion Prayer

God of this joyful table, you gather us in to remember the past but not to dwell in it. In the words of Jesus and the blessing of bread and wine, we recall who we are and what you have done for us, and we find all that we need to live faithfully right now. For your wonders that are new and becoming, we give you thanks. Transform us in your love and by your grace, renewed for the ministry of the gospel for our time. Amen.

FOURTH SUNDAY OF ADVENT

Call to Worship

One: Lord, we are ready and waiting!

**All: The tree might not be perfect,
the gifts may not be wrapped,
the house is still a mess,
but Lord, we are ready!**

One: The earth cries out for a savior,
and we are waiting for love to be born.

**All: All is not calm, all is not bright . . .
we are so ready for love to live among us
in the flesh.**

One: Come as you are, says the Lord.
Arise and shine, for your light is coming.

**All: Come, Lord Jesus. We may not be
prepared, but we are ready.
Let your light of love shine
in the darkness.**

Candle-Lighting Liturgy and Children's Time

Today is the Fourth Sunday of Advent. Who remembers what we are waiting for during this Advent time? (*Shout, "Christmas!" if the children need help.*)

Yes, and it is almost time for Jesus to be born. It is almost Christmas! And because it's almost Christmas, I know what many of us are also waiting for. (*Help the children by saying, "presents" if they didn't say presents the first time.*) Yes, presents!

And that is important too. Who wants to tell us something you are hoping to get for Christmas?

(Let the kids share some of what they have asked Santa for; or if you don't want to mention Santa, just asked for in general. Remember to avoid Santa spoilers either way! Once they have shared something from their wish list, maybe share something you hope to receive.)

We all have things we are hoping to find under the tree, but do you know what I wish for you? I wish that each of you will get at least one surprise! Something totally unexpected. Because we learn as we get older that some of our best gifts are things that people give us out of love and thoughtfulness, things that we would never have thought about asking or wishing for ourselves!

Of course, the greatest gift we are all waiting for is baby Jesus, who will be born to love the world and to show us how to love the world. We remember that when Jesus was born, it was a big surprise for everyone! God continues to surprise us with love, and we are thankful.

Reader 1: I will tell of the kindnesses of the
                    LORD,
                the deeds for which he is to be
                    praised,
                according to all the LORD has done
                    for us —
            yes, the many good things
                he has done for Israel,
                according to his compassion and
                    many kindnesses.
            He said, "Surely they are my people,
                children who will be true to me";
                and so he became their Savior.

In all their distress he too was
distressed,
    and the angel of his presence saved
them.
In his love and mercy he redeemed
them;
    he lifted them up and carried them
all the days of old.[6]

Reader 2: Today we light the candle of love. God created the world, and God so loved the world that he didn't want to love it from far off anymore. It was love that made us and love that brought God to live with us, live and in person. Love still lights the way.

Reader 3: Let us pray: Dear God, are we doing this right? Sometimes we aren't sure. We think that we are ready for the baby to be born who will lead us in love. Show us how to love our neighbors while we wait. As we welcome the baby Jesus to the world, teach us how to also be like him. Let the light of your love live in us for all to see. Amen.

Communion Prayer

Gather us as beloved family at your table, Lord. May the light of love stand at the center as a reminder of all that we have and all that we are; may the same light carry us out to the world with bread for all. Amen.

CHRISTMAS EVE

Call to Worship

One: What kind of hope can endure
this world?

**All: The hopes and fears of all the years
are met right here tonight.**

One: How can we speak peace when the world
is at war?

**All: Tonight, there will be heavenly peace
and mercy mild; God and sinners,
reconciled.**

One: Where is the joy of celebration
when so many are hungry and hurting?

**All: All heaven and nature sing;
the weary world rejoices.**

One: When will love come and save us?

**All: The wonders of God's love are made
flesh tonight. The angels sing "gloria,"
and we have nothing to fear.**

Welcoming the Light into the World

The Light of Hope
Scripture Reading: Isaiah 11:1–9
Reflection: With the candle of hope, we light the way for those who will come after us, just as the prophets before lit the path for us. We carry the light as we journey to Bethlehem. The child of hope brings good news for the world; news of hope endures through all fear.

The Light of Peace
Scripture Reading: Luke 1:46–56
Reflection: This is the light of peace, to honor the child who will teach us the way. Mary knew that her baby would be the one to end all war. We witness to the light, doing our part to create a nonviolent world. We welcome the Prince of Peace, who casts out all fear.

The Light of Joy
Scripture Reading: Psalm 118:1–7, 22–24
Reflection: A flame of joy flickers and grows against the darkness. It burns brightest when we are together. God's joy comes to live among us, and in the longest, darkest nights, we find joy that releases us from fear.

The Light of Love
Scripture Reading: Luke 2:1–7
Reflection: The light of love always shows the way. For the holy family on a dark night in Bethlehem, and for all who come to worship the child, who is God with us. Love still shows us where to go: a way where there is no way and a light of love that knows no fear.

The Christ Candle
Scripture Reading: Luke 2:8–20
Reflection: We welcome hope, peace, joy, and love tonight. The light of the world is born, bringing all that and more! It is a light for the ages. God's people answer the call to keep the light and shine it for all to see. The light shines in the darkness, and the darkness does not overcome it.

Christmas Prayer for a Weary World

God of hope, Joyful Spirit, Prince of Peace
and Lord of Love, we wait for you to come
live among us. Tonight we learn a new name
for you: God with us, Immanuel. It is as old
as the ages and as new as a newborn baby's
cry. We wait, believing what all your prophets told us is true: that your grace is sufficient
and that your love will transform the world.

The world is a weary world, and we are
tired of waiting. We trust and we hope, but
we are also tired. We don't know if we're
doing this right, and we are so often afraid.
We pray for angels to deliver and to comfort
us. We long to hear spoken again those words
of assurance, your messenger's commandment, "do not be afraid."

Give us courage for these times, Lord:
for the long nights of winter, for the darkness of human chaos and suffering, and for
the brokenness of our own imperfect selves.
Empower us, by your grace and in your spirit,
to live as those who long for your saving love—
and as those who keep your light, even while
we wait.

Send your strength and renew our faith,
Lord. Be in our midst tonight, in the candles
that we hold and the bread that we break,
in the stories that we share and speak and
sing. Come to us as an answered prayer and
a long-awaited hope; be among us in ways
seen and unseen.

For all the joy of these days, we still lift our lights against present darkness. We pray tonight for neighbors who are cold and hungry, for those who are alone and those who would rather be alone than in houses of violence. We pray for those around the world who live in perilous conflict or in crippling poverty. Lord, hear our prayer: for the prisoner and the immigrant, for the child in foster care, and for the elderly widow with no living family; for those in addiction recovery and for those still trapped by the power of substance. Lord, hear our prayer for a world groaning under the weight of greed, of climate change, of growing natural disasters.

Against all the darkness of the world and the cruel cold of winter, we dare to believe that all you've promised is true. That you stepped into human form and came to dwell among us; that the story we tell tonight will breathe hope, peace, joy, and love into all the hurting places we can name. Give us ears to hear again the good news of your word made flesh, and come to life in our midst. Can you show us again what it is to be your people in such a world, how to carry the word of your prophets and the light of your love to the places that seem the hardest to reach? Can you lead us again in the way of transformation that will not be hindered by human failure? Can you tell us again your story of the impossible dream that comes true when we are bold enough to believe?

Guide us and keep us, Lord. As you step into our world again, may you find your people ready. Amen.

Communion Prayer

We remember, every time we gather at the Communion table:
That the disruption is the point.
That God came to the world as a baby to disrupt the powerful and lift up the poor.
To let the last be first.
To take the sting out of death.
And to make a place where every stranger would be a welcomed guest.
Once Jesus had celebrated a few birthdays, he set the table for his friends and he told them that, in spite of all that was to come, they didn't have to be afraid.
(*Share the words of institution per your tradition.*)
Let us pray . . .

God of the crowded table, we welcome you this night as a beloved guest, as you have gathered each of us in from near and far. Bless this bread and cup to renew and restore us, your body of Christ for the weary world. Amen.

ADVENT PLAYLIST

Find this "Calling All Angels" playlist on Spotify at:
https://spoti.fi/3K230It

"Calling All Angels" by The Wailin' Jennys
"O Come, O Come Emmanuel" by the Civil Wars
"Peace Child" by the Indigo Girls
"Come Darkness, Come Light" by Mary Chapin Carpenter
"Gabriel's Message" by Sting
"The Trumpet Child" by Over the Rhine
"There's a Light" by Emmylou Harris
"Who Comes This Night" by James Taylor
"They Sang Silent Night" by Fiona Bevin
"Angels We Have Heard on High, Remastered 2006" by Ella Fitzgerald
"Born" by Over the Rhine
"O Little Town of Bethlehem" by Emmylou Harris
"Better Days" by the Goo Goo Dolls
"Hark! The Herald Angels Sing" by Amy Grant
"Someday at Christmas" by Stevie Wonder

"Christmas Must Be Tonight" by the Band
"Angels from the Realms of Glory" by Annie
    Lennox
"Let It Be, Remastered 2009" by The Beatles
"Guiding Light" by Mumford & Sons
"Heaven & Earth" by Leslie Odom Jr.
"In the Bleak Midwinter" by Indigo Girls

NOTES

First Week of Advent

1. Fred B. Craddock, *Luke*, Interpretation: A Bible Commentary for Teaching and Preaching (Louisville, KY: Westminster John Knox Press, Louisville, 1990), 26–31.

2. David Albert Jones, *Angels: A Very Short Introduction* (New York: Oxford University Press, 2011), 50–51.

3. Thomas Merton, *Choosing to Love the World* (Boulder, CO: Sounds True Publishing, 2015), 101.

4. Louis F. Benson, "O Little Town of Bethlehem," *Studies of Familiar Hymns* (Philadelphia: The Westminster Press, 1924), 5.

Second Week of Advent

1. Courtney V. Buggs, "Commentary on Luke 1:26–38," Working Preacher, https://www.working preacher.org/commentaries/revised-common -lectionary/fourth-sunday-of-advent-2 /commentary-on-luke-126-38-5.

2. Raj Nadella, "Commentary on Luke 1:26–38,"

Working Preacher, https://www.workingpreacher
.org/commentaries/revised-common-lectionary
/fourth-sunday-of-advent-2/commentary-on-luke
-126-38-6.

3. *Magnificat* print, Ben Wildflower Art, https://
benwildflower.com/products/magnificat-print.

4. Martin Luther King Jr., "Letter from Bir-
mingham Jail," African Studies Center, University of Pennsylvania, https://www.africa.upenn
.edu/Articles_Gen/Letter_Birmingham.html.

5. Isabel Wilkerson, *Caste: The Origins of Our Discontent* (New York: Random House, 2020), 99.

6. bell hooks, "Building a Community of Love:
bell hooks and Thich Nhat Hanh," Lion's Roar:
Buddhist Wisdom for Our Times, https://www
.lionsroar.com/bell-hooks-and-thich-nhat-hanh
-on-building-a-community-of-love/.

7. hooks, "Building a Community of Love."

8. Stevie Wonder, "Someday at Christmastime,"
Someday at Christmas, Motown Records, 1967.

9. Wonder, "Someday at Christmastime."

Third Week of Advent

1. Alyce M. McKenzie, *Matthew*, Interpretation
Bible Studies (Louisville, KY: Westminster John
Knox Press, 2002), 2–3.

2. McKenzie, 13.

3. Parker J. Palmer, "Bringing Christmas Back
Down to Earth," On Being, https://onbeing.org
/blog/bringing-christmas-back-down-to-earth/.

4. Theodore Roethke, *Straw for the Fire: From the
Notebooks of Theodore Roethke*, ed. David Wagoner (Port
Townsend, WA: Copper Canyon Press, 2006), 40.

5. Leonard Cohen, "Anthem." The Future, Columbia, 1992.

Fourth Week of Advent

1. Eric C. Smith, "No Place in the Guest Room," A Lover's Quarrel, https://ericcsmith.substack.com/p /no-place-in-the-guest-room?utm_source=post -email-title&publication_id=1028605&post _id=140036779&utm_campaign=email-post-title&i sFreemail=true&r=e0wr3&utm_medium=email.

2. Emmylou Harris, vocalist, "There's a Light," by Beth Nielsen Chapman, *Light of the Stable*, Warner Brothers, 2002.

3. Angel Kocherga, "Migrants Warmed by the Community as Freezing Temperatures Linger in El Paso," National Public Radio, https://www .npr.org/2022/12/24/1145245308/el-paso-migrants -church-shelters-christmas-freezing.

4. Kevin Beaty, "A Run-Down Motel Became an Accidental Sanctuary for Hundreds of Migrants. In Them, Its Owner Found Renewed Purpose and Meaning," Denverite, https://denverite.com/2023/12 /22/a-run-down-motel-became-an-accidental -sanctuary-for-hundreds-of-migrants-in-them -its-owner-found-renewed-purpose-and -meaning/?utm_campaign=later-linkinbio-npr &utm_content=later-40045393&utm _medium=social&utm_source=linkin.bio.

5. Beaty, "A Run-Down Motel."

Christmas

1. Fiona Bevin, "They Sang Silent Night," *They Sang Silent Night*, Navigator Records, 2014.

2. Michael Ray, "Christmas Truce: World War I," Britannica, https://www.britannica.com/event /The-Christmas-Truce.

3. Kelly Latimore, "Christ in the Rubble," https://kellylatimoreicons.com/?fbclid=IwAR2FPz eT09y365xsCORgFlhbeXamxn -VEJzugtlTq0Zr -fn73bFTQ69OBJk.

4. "Trump Administration Sets Record Low Limit for New U.S. Refugees," Reuters, https:// www.reuters.com/article/idUSKBN27D1UG/.

5. Susan Hartman, "How Refugees Transformed a Dying Rust Belt Town," *New York Times*, June 3, 2022, https://www.nytimes.com/interactive/2022/06 /03/realestate/utica-burma-refugees.html.

6. Mallory Moench, "Bethlehem Reverend Delivers 'Christ in the Rubble' Christmas Sermon amid Gaza Conflict," *Time Magazine*, https://www .time.com/6550851/bethlehem-christmas -sermon-nativity-rubble/.

7. Moench, "Bethlehem Reverend Delivers."

Worship Resources
1. Based on Habakkuk 2 and Zechariah 2.
2. Psalm 27:1, 4–5, 13–14.
3. Isaiah 9:2–4, 6.
4. Based on Isaiah 43.
5. Jeremiah 30:10–11a.
6. Isaiah 63:7–9, NIV.

Printed in the USA
CPSIA information can be obtained
at www.ICGtesting.com
CBHW051056200824
13316CB00006B/6

9 780664 268978